ALL'S WELL THAT ENDS WELL

ALL'S WELL THAT ENDS WELL

Charles Dickens

WORDSWORTH CLASSICS

The paper in this book is produced from pure wood
pulp, without the use of chlorine or any other substance
harmful to the environment. The energy used in its
production consists almost entirely of hydroelectricity
and heat generated from waste materials, thereby
conserving fossil fuels and contributing little to the
greenhouse effect.

This edition published 1994 by
Wordsworth Editions Limited
Cumberland House, Crib Street, Ware,
Hertfordshire SG12 9ET

ISBN 1 85326 205 4

Printed and bound in Denmark by Nørhaven
Typeset in the UK by The R & B Partnership

INTRODUCTION

All's Well that Ends Well (circa 1602) eludes definitive classification as a Comedy, History or Tragedy. It also has a close affinity with *Measure for Measure*, both plays forming part of Shakespeare's later work and they have been variously described as tragi-comedies, problem comedies or dark comedies. There is an enigmatic quality to *All's Well that Ends Well* and it has been categorised as being 'crude enough to be early, yet mature enough to be late.' Indeed, it is only in recent years that scholars have agreed on the position of *All's Well that Ends Well* as being a work of Shakespeare's maturity. The inspiration for the play was almost certainly Boccaccio's *Decameron*. The story concerns Bertram, the young Count of Rousillon, who on his father's death is summoned to the court of the King of France, leaving behind him his mother and the heroine Helena, daughter of the famous physician Gerard de Narbon.

The King of France is suffering from a disease widely thought of as being incurable. However, Helena who loves the courtier Bertram, travels to Paris and effects a cure for the king by means of a prescription left by her father. As a reward, she is permitted to choose her husband and she selects Bertram who unwillingly obeys the king's order to marry her. Under the malign influence of the worthless braggart Parolles, Bertram enters the service of the Duke of Florence and informs Helena that until she can remove the ring from his finger and bear his child he will not return to her and neither may she call herself his wife. Helena disguises herself as a pilgrim and travels to Florence where she finds Bertram courting Diana, the daughter of her hostess in Florence. Helena discloses her true identity to the host family and takes Diana's place at a secret assignation with Bertram having put about the story that she (Helena) is dead. Helena exchanges rings with Bertram, giving him the king's ring, and conceives a child by Bertram. The King of France, on a visit to the house of Bertram's mother, recognises his ring and accuses Bertram of killing Helena, of whom he is very fond, and demands an explanation on pain of death. Helena then appears and reveals the truth of her masquerade as Diana and explains that Bertram's conditions have now been met. The stage is then set for the classic Shakespearean *finale* in which the remorseful

Bertram accepts Helena as his loving wife. *All's Well that Ends Well* is a problem play at many levels; there is the difficulty in feeling sympathy for Bertram, and in taking real pleasure in Helena's success, as her character is not as developed as many of the leading women in Shakespeare's plays. There are many similarities with Mariana and Angelo in *Measure for Measure*. Helena's mother, on the other hand, is one of Shakespeare's great creations. The subplot concerning Parolles is regarded by many as being one of the most successful and dominant aspects of the play both on the page and on the stage.

Details of Shakespeare's early life are scanty. He was the son of a prosperous merchant of Stratford-upon-Avon, and tradition has it that he was born on 23rd April 1564; records show that he was baptised three days later. It is likely that he attended the local grammar school, but he had no university education. Of his early career there is no record, though John Aubrey states that he was, for a time, a country schoolmaster. How he became involved with the stage is equally uncertain, but he was sufficiently established as a playwright by 1592 to be criticised in print. He was a leading member of the Lord Chamberlain's Company, which became the King's Men on the accession of James I in 1603. Shakespeare married Anne Hathaway in 1582, by whom he had two daughters and a son, Hamnet, who died in childhood. Towards the end of his life he loosened his ties with London, and retired to New Place, his substantial property in Stratford that he had bought in 1597. He died on 23rd April 1616 aged 52, and is buried in Holy Trinity Church, Stratford.

Further reading:
R Berman: A Reader's Guide to Shakespeare's Plays 1973
R A Foakes: Shakespeare: The Dark Comedies to the Last Plays 1971
W W Lawrence: Shakespeare's Problem Comedies 1931; 1969
K Muir (ed): Shakespeare The Comedies 1965

ALL'S WELL THAT ENDS WELL

The scene: Rousillon, Paris, Florence,
Marseilles

CHARACTERS IN THE PLAY

KING OF FRANCE

DUKE OF FLORENCE

BERTRAM, *the young Count of Rousillon*

LAFEU, *an old lord*

PAROLLES, *a follower of Bertram*

RINALDO, *Steward to the Countess of Rousillon*

LAVACHE, *Clown to the Countess*

Two French gentlemen at Court named DUMAIN,
later captains in the Florentine army

A soldier, pretending to be an interpreter

A gentleman, astringer to the French king

A Page

COUNTESS OF ROUSILLON, *mother to Bertram*

HELENA, *a waiting-gentlewoman to the Countess*

A Widow of Florence

DIANA, *daughter to the widow*

MARIANA, *neighbour to the widow*

Lords, officers, soldiers, &c., French and Florentine

ALL'S WELL
THAT ENDS WELL

[I. I.]   *A room in the palace of Rousillon*

Enter BERTRAM *the young Count of Rousillon, his
mother the* COUNTESS, HELENA, *and Lord* LAFEU, '*all
in black*'

Countess. In delivering my son from me I bury a
second husband.

Bertram. And I in going, madam, weep o'er my
father's death anew: but I must attend his majesty's
command, to whom I am now in ward, evermore in
subjection.

Lafeu. You shall find of the king a husband, madam—
you, sir, a father. He that so generally is at all times
good, must of necessity hold his virtue to you, whose
worthiness would stir it up where it wanted rather than 10
lack it where there is such abundance.

Countess. What hope is there of his majesty's amend-
ment?

Lafeu. He hath abandoned his physicians, madam,
under whose practices he hath persecuted time with
hope, and finds no other advantage in the process but
only the losing of hope by time.

Countess. This young gentlewoman had a father—
O, that 'had,' how sad a passage 'tis—whose skill was
almost as great as his honesty; had it stretched so far, 20
would have made nature immortal, and death should
have play for lack of work. Would, for the king's sake,
he were living. I think it would be the death of the
king's disease.

Lafeu. How called you the man you speak of, madam?

Countess. He was famous, sir, in his profession, and it was his great right to be so: Gerard de Narbon.

Lafeu. He was excellent, indeed, madam. The king 30 very lately spoke of him admiringly and mourningly: he was skilful enough to have lived still, if knowledge could be set up against mortality.

Bertram. What is it, my good lord, the king languishes of?

Lafeu. A fistula, my lord.

Bertram. I heard not of it before.

Lafeu. I would it were not notorious....Was this gentlewoman the daughter of Gerard de Narbon?

Countess. His sole child, my lord, and bequeathed to 40 my overlooking. I have those hopes of her good that her education promises: her dispositions she inherits, which make fair gifts fairer; for where an unclean mind carries virtuous qualities, there commendations go with pity, they are virtues and traitors too; in her they are the better for their simpleness; she derives her honesty and achieves her goodness.

Lafeu. Your commendations, madam, get from her tears.

Countess. 'Tis the best brine a maiden can season her 50 praise in. The remembrance of her father never approaches her heart but the tyranny of her sorrows takes all livelihood from her cheek....No more of this, Helena, go to, no more, lest it be rather thought you affect a sorrow than to have—

Helena. I do affect a sorrow indeed, but I have it too.

Lafeu. †How understand we that? Moderate lamentation is the right of the dead, excessive grief the enemy to the living.

Countess. If the living be enemy to the grief, the excess
makes it soon mortal.   60
Bertram. Madam, I desire your holy wishes.
Countess. Be thou blest, Bertram, and succeed
     thy father
In manners as in shape: thy blood and virtue
Contend for empire in thee, and thy goodness
Share with thy birthright. Love all, trust a few,
Do wrong to none: be able for thine enemy
Rather in power than use; and keep thy friend
Under thy own life's key: be checked for silence,
But never taxed for speech....What heaven more will,
That thee may furnish, and my prayers pluck down,   70
Fall on thy head....[*she kisses him*] Farewell, my lord.
      [*she turns to go, passing Lafeu on the way*
'Tis an unseasoned courtier. Good my lord,
Advise him.
Lafeu.   He cannot want the best
†That shall attend his lord.
Countess. Heaven bless him! Farewell, Bertram.
      [*she departs*
Bertram. The best wishes that can be forged in your
thoughts be servants to you! [*to Helena*] Be comfortable
to my mother, your mistress, and make much of her.
Lafeu. Farewell, pretty lady, you must hold the credit
of your father.   80
     [*Bertram and Lafeu go out by another door*
Helena. O, were that all! I think not on my father,
And these great tears grace his remembrance more
Than those I shed for him. What was he like?
I have forgot him: my imagination
Carries no favour in't but Bertram's....
I am undone, there is no living, none,
If Bertram be away....'Twere all one

That I should love a bright particular star,
And think to wed it, he is so above me:
90 In his bright radiance and collateral light
Must I be comforted, not in his sphere....
Th'ambition in my love thus plagues itself:
The hind that would be mated by the lion
Must die for love. 'Twas pretty, though a plague,
To see him every hour, to sit and draw
His archéd brows, his hawking eye, his curls,
In our heart's table; heart too capable
Of every line and trick of his sweet favour....
But now he's gone, and my idolatrous fancy
100 Must sanctify his relics. Who comes here?

PAROLLES *enters*

One that goes with him: I love him for his sake,
And yet I know him a notorious liar,
Think him a great way fool, solely a coward.
Yet these fixed evils sit so fit in him,
That they take place, when virtue's steely bones
Look bleak i'th' cold wind: withal, full oft we see
Cold wisdom waiting on superfluous folly.
    Parolles. Save you, fair queen.
    Helena. And you, monarch.
110 *Parolles.* No.
    Helena. And no.
    Parolles. Are you meditating on virginity?
    Helena. Ay...You have some stain of soldier in you;
let me ask you a question. Man is enemy to virginity,
how may we barricado it against him?
    Parolles. Keep him out.
    Helena. But he assails, and our virginity, though
valiant in the defence, yet is weak: unfold to us some
warlike resistance.

Parolles. There is none: man, setting down before 120
you, will undermine you and blow you up.

Helena. Bless our poor virginity from underminers
and blowers up! Is there no military policy, how
virgins might blow up men?

Parolles. Virginity being blown down, man will
quicklier be blown up: marry, in blowing him down
again, with the breach yourselves made, you lose your
city. It is not politic in the commonwealth of nature to
preserve virginity. Loss of virginity is rational increase,
and there was never virgin got till virginity was first lost. 130
That you were made of is mettle to make virgins.
Virginity by being once lost may be ten times found:
by being ever kept, it is ever lost: 'tis too cold a companion: away with't!

Helena. I will stand for't a little, though therefore
I die a virgin.

Parolles. There's little can be said in't—'tis against the
rule of nature. To speak on the part of virginity, is to
accuse your mothers; which is most infallible dis-
obedience. He that hangs himself is a virgin: virginity 140
murders itself, and should be buried in highways out
of all sanctified limit, as a desperate offendress against
nature. Virginity breeds mites—much like a cheese—
consumes itself to the very paring, and so dies with
feeding his own stomach. Besides, virginity is peevish,
proud, idle, made of self-love, which is the most inhibited sin in the canon. Keep it not—you cannot choose
but lose by't. Out with't: within ten year it will make
itself ten, which is a goodly increase—and the principal
itself not much the worse. Away with't.   150

Helena. How might one do, sir, to lose it to her own
liking?

Parolles. Let me see. Marry, ill, to like him that ne'er

it likes. 'Tis a commodity will lose the gloss with lying;
the longer kept, the less worth: off with't while 'tis
vendible; answer the time of request. Virginity, like
an old courtier, wears her cap out of fashion, richly
suited, but unsuitable, just like the brooch and the tooth-
pick, which wear not now...Your date is better in your
160 pie and your porridge than in your cheek: and your
virginity, your old virginity, is like one of our French
withered pears, it looks ill, it eats drily, marry 'tis a
withered pear; it was formerly better, marry yet 'tis
a withered pear: will you any thing with it?
    Helena. †Not my virginity yet...
There shall your master have a thousand loves,
A mother, and a mistress, and a friend,
A phœnix, captain, and an enemy,
A guide, a goddess, and a sovereign,
170 A counsellor, a traitress, and a dear;
His humble ambition, proud humility:
His jarring concord, and his discord dulcet:
His faith, his sweet disaster; with a world
Of pretty, fond, adoptious christendoms,
That blinking Cupid gossips. Now shall he...
I know not what he shall. God send him well!
The court's a learning place, and he is one—
    Parolles. What one, i' faith?
    Helena. That I wish well. 'Tis pity—
180 *Parolles.* What's pity?
    Helena. That wishing well had not a body in't,
Which might be felt, that we, the poorer born,
Whose baser stars do shut us up in wishes,
Might with effects of them follow our friends,
And show what we alone must think, which never
Returns us thanks.

A page enters

Page. Monsieur Parolles, my lord calls for you.

                                                      [he goes

Parolles. Little Helen, farewell. If I can remember thee, I will think of thee at court.

Helena. Monsieur Parolles, you were born under a 190 charitable star.

Parolles. Under Mars, I.

Helena. I especially think, under Mars.

Parolles. Why under Mars?

Helena. The wars have so kept you under, that you must needs be born under Mars.

Parolles. When he was predominant.

Helena. When he was retrograde, I think, rather.

Parolles. Why think you so?

Helena. You go so much backward when you fight. 200

Parolles. That's for advantage.

Helena. So is running away, when fear proposes the safety: but the composition that your valour and fear makes in you is a virtue of a good wing, and I like the wear well.

Parolles. I am so full of businesses, I cannot answer thee acutely: I will return perfect courtier, in the which my instruction shall serve to naturalize thee, so thou wilt be capable of a courtier's counsel, and understand what advice shall thrust upon thee—else thou diest in thine 210 unthankfulness, and thine ignorance makes thee away. Farewell: when thou hast leisure, say thy prayers; when thou hast †money, remember thy friends: get thee a good husband, and use him as he uses thee: so farewell.

                                                      [he goes

Helena. Our remedies oft in ourselves do lie,
Which we ascribe to heaven: the fated sky

Gives us free scope; only doth backward pull
Our slow designs when we ourselves are dull.
What power is it which mounts my love so high?
220 That makes me see, and cannot feed mine eye?
The mightiest space in fortune nature brings
To join like likes, and kiss like native things.
Impossible be strange attempts to those
That weigh their pains in sense, and do suppose
What hath been cannot be: who ever strove
To show her merit that did miss her love?
The king's disease—my project may deceive me,
But my intents are fixed, and will not leave me.

                                        [*she goes*

[1. 2.]   *A room in the King's palace at Paris*

A flourish of cornets: the KING OF FRANCE *enters supported by attendants, lords and councillors following; he sits in the chair of state and letters are placed before him*

   King. The Florentines and Senoys are by th'ears,
Have fought with equal fortune, and continue
A braving war.
   1 *Lord.*   So 'tis reported, sir.
   King. Nay, 'tis most credible. We here receive it
A certainty, vouched from our cousin Austria,
With caution, that the Florentine will move us
For speedy aid; wherein our dearest friend
Prejudicates the business, and would seem
To have us make denial.
   1 *Lord.*   His love and wisdom,
10 Approved so to your majesty, may plead
For amplest credence.
   King.   He hath armed our answer,
And Florence is denied before he comes:
Yet, for our gentlemen that mean to see

The Tuscan service, freely have they leave
To stand on either part.

2 Lord.   It well may serve
A nursery to our gentry, who are sick
For breathing and exploit.

BERTRAM, LAFEU, and PAROLLES enter the chamber

King.   What's he comes here?

1 Lord. It is the Count Rousillon, my good lord,
Young Bertram.

King.   Youth, thou bear'st thy father's face.
Frank nature, rather curious than in haste,   20
Hath well composed thee: thy father's moral parts
Mayst thou inherit too! Welcome to Paris.

Bertram. My thanks and duty are your majesty's.

King. I would I had that corporal soundness now,
As when thy father and myself in friendship
First tried our soldiership! He did look far
Into the service of the time, and was
Discipled of the bravest: he lasted long,
But on us both did haggish age steal on,
And wore us out of act...It much repairs me   30
To talk of your good father...In his youth
He had the wit, which I can well observe
To-day in our young lords; but they may jest
Till their own scorn return to them unnoted
Ere they can hide their levity in honour:
So like a courtier, contempt nor bitterness
Were in his pride or sharpness; if they were,
His equal had awaked them, and his honour,
Clock to itself, knew the true minute when
Exception bid him speak, and at this time   40
His tongue obeyed his hand. Who were below him
He used as creatures of another place,

And bowed his eminent top to their low ranks,
Making them proud of his humility,
†In their poor praise he humble...Such a man
Might be a copy to these younger times;
Which, followed well, would demonstrate them now
But goers backward.
   Bertram.   His good remembrance, sir,
Lies richer in your thoughts than on his tomb;
50 So in approof lives not his epitaph
As in your royal speech.
   King. Would I were with him! He would
       always say—
Methinks I hear him now; his plausive words
He scattered not in ears, but grafted them,
To grow there, and to bear—'Let me not live,'—
Thus his good melancholy oft began,
On the catastrophe and heel of pastime,
When it was out—'Let me not live,' quoth he,
'After my flame lacks oil, to be the snuff
60 Of younger spirits, whose apprehensive senses
All but new things disdain; whose judgements are
Mere fathers of their garments; whose constancies
Expire before their fashions'...This he wished:
I after him do after him wish too,
Since I nor wax nor honey can bring home,
I quickly were dissolvéd from my hive,
To give some labourers room.
   2 *Lord.*   You are loved, sir,
They that least lend it you shall lack you first.
   King. I fill a place, I know't....How long is't, count,
70 Since the physician at your father's died?
He was much famed.
   Bertram.   Some six months since, my lord.
   King. If he were living, I would try him yet.

Lend me an arm...the rest have worn me out
With several applications: nature and sickness
Debate it at their leisure. Welcome, count,
My son's no dearer.

Bertram.   Thank your majesty.

*The King departs with a flourish of trumpets;
the court follows*

[1. 3.]   *A room in the palace of Rousillon*

The COUNTESS *enters with* RINALDO *her Steward;*
LAVACHE *the Clown follows behind*

Countess. I will now hear. What say you of this
gentlewoman?

Steward [*observes the Clown*]. Madam, the care I
have had to even your content, I wish might be found
in the calendar of my past endeavours, for then we
wound our modesty, and make foul the clearness of our
deservings, when of ourselves we publish them.

Countess [*understands*]. What does this knave here?
Get you gone, sirrah: the complaints I have heard of
you I do not all believe: 'tis my slowness that I do not: 10
for I know you lack not folly to commit them, and have
ability enough to make such knaveries yours.

Clown. 'Tis not unknown to you, madam, I am a
poor fellow.

Countess. Well, sir.

Clown. No, madam, 'tis not so well that I am poor,
though many of the rich are damned, but, if I may have
your ladyship's good will to go to the world, Isbel the
woman and I will do as we may.

Countess. Wilt thou needs be a beggar?   20

Clown. I do beg your good will in this case.

Countess. In what case?

2   PSAW

Clown. In Isbel's case and mine own...Service is no heritage, and I think I shall never have the blessing of God till I have issue o' my body: for they say barnes are blessings.

Countess. Tell me thy reason why thou wilt marry.

Clown. My poor body, madam, requires it. I am driven on by the flesh, and he must needs go that the devil drives.

30 *Countess.* Is this all your worship's reason?

Clown. Faith, madam, I have other holy reasons, such as they are.

Countess. May the world know them?

Clown. I have been, madam, a wicked creature, as you and all flesh and blood are, and indeed I do marry that I may repent.

Countess. Thy marriage, sooner than thy wickedness.

Clown. I am out o' friends, madam, and I hope to have friends for my wife's sake.

40 *Countess.* Such friends are thine enemies, knave.

Clown. Y'are shallow, madam, in great friends, for the knaves come to do that for me, which I am aweary of...He that ears my land spares my team, and gives me leave to inn the crop: if I be his cuckold he's my drudge; he that comforts my wife is the cherisher of my flesh and blood; he that cherishes my flesh and blood loves my flesh and blood; he that loves my flesh and blood is my friend: ergo, he that kisses my wife is my friend...If men could be contented to be what they

50 are, there were no fear in marriage; for young Chairbonne the puritan and old Poisson the papist, howsome'er their hearts are severed in religion, their heads are both one—they may jowl horns together like any deer i'th' herd.

Countess. Wilt thou ever be a foul-mouthed and calumnious knave?

Clown. A prophet I, madam, and I speak the truth
the next way—
      For I the ballad will repeat,
        Which men full true shall find,   60
      Your marriage comes by destiny,
        Your cuckoo sings by kind.

Countess. Get you gone, sir. I'll talk with you more
anon.

Steward. May it please you, madam, that he bid
Helen come to you. Of her I am to speak.

Countess. Sirrah, tell my gentlewoman I would speak
with her—Helen I mean.

Clown [*sings*]. Was this fair face the cause, quoth she,
      Why the Grecians sackéd Troy?   70
      Fond done, done fond,
        Was this King Priam's joy?
      With that she sighéd as she stood,
      With that she sighéd as she stood,
        And gave this sentence then—
      Among nine bad if one be good,
      Among nine bad if one be good,
        There's yet one good in ten.

Countess. What, one good in ten? you corrupt the
song, sirrah.   80

Clown. One good woman in ten, madam, which is
a purifying o'th' song: would God would serve the
world so all the year! we'd find no fault with the tithe-
woman, if I were the parson. One in ten, quoth a'! an
we might have a good woman born but or every blazing
star, or at an earthquake, 'twould mend the lottery well
—a man may draw his heart out, ere a' pluck one.

Countess. You'll be gone, sir knave, and do as I command you!

Clown. That man should be at woman's command, 90

and yet no hurt done! Though honesty be no puritan, yet it will do no hurt; it will wear the surplice of humility over the black gown of a big heart....[*the Countess stamps her foot*] I am going, forsooth. The business is for Helen to come hither.   [*he goes*

Countess. Well, now.

Steward. I know, madam, you love your gentlewoman entirely.

Countess. Faith, I do: her father bequeathed her to
100 me, and she herself, without other advantage, may lawfully make title to as much love as she finds. There is more owing her than is paid, and more shall be paid her than she'll demand.

Steward. Madam, I was very late more near her than I think she wished me. Alone she was, and did communicate to herself her own words to her own ears. She thought, I dare vow for her, they touched not any stranger sense. Her matter was, she loved your son: Fortune, she said, was no goddess, that had put such
110 difference betwixt their two estates; Love no god, that would not extend his might, only where qualities were level; †Diana no queen of virgins, that would suffer her poor knight surprised, without rescue in the first assault, or ransom afterward...This she delivered in the most bitter touch of sorrow that e'er I heard virgin exclaim in, which I held my duty speedily to acquaint you withal, sithence in the loss that may happen it concerns you something to know it.

Countess. You have discharged this honestly, keep
120 it to yourself. Many likelihoods informed me of this before, which hung so tott'ring in the balance, that I could neither believe nor misdoubt...Pray you, leave me. Stall this in your bosom, and I thank you for your honest care: I will speak with you further anon. [*he goes*

*HELENA enters by another door and stands
awaiting her mistress's will*

[*aside*] Even so it was with me, when I was young...
    If ever we are nature's, these are ours. This thorn
Doth to our rose of youth rightly belong.
    Our blood to us, this to our blood is born.
It is the show and seal of nature's truth,
Where love's strong passion is impressed in youth.   130
By our remembrances of days foregone,
Such were our faults, or then we thought them none.
                    [*she beckons Helena to draw near*
Her eye is sick on't—I observe her now.
  Helena. What is your pleasure, madam?
  Countess.   You know, Helen,
I am a mother to you.
  Helena. Mine honourable mistress.
  Countess.   Nay, a mother.
Why not a mother? When I said 'a mother'
Methought you saw a serpent. What's in 'mother,'
That you start at it? I say, I am your mother,
And put you in the catalogue of those   140
That were enwombéd mine. 'Tis often seen
Adoption strives with nature, and choice breeds
A native slip to us from foreign seeds:
You ne'er oppressed me with a mother's groan,
Yet I express to you a mother's care—
God's mercy, maiden! does it curd thy blood
To say I am thy mother? What's the matter,
That this distempered messenger of wet,
The many-coloured Iris, rounds thine eye?
Why? that you are my daughter?
  Helena.   That I am not.   150
  Countess. I say, I am your mother.

Helena.   Pardon, madam;
The Count Rousillon cannot be my brother:
I am from humble, he from honoured name;
No note upon my parents, his all noble.
My master, my dear lord he is, and I
His servant live, and will his vassal die:
He must not be my brother.
    Countess.   Nor I your mother?
    Helena. You are my mother, madam. Would
      you were—
So that my lord, your son, were not my brother—
160 Indeed my mother! or were you both our mothers.
†I care no more for't than I do for heaven,
So I were not his sister. Can't no other,
But I your daughter, he must be my brother?
    Countess. Yes, Helen, you might be my daughter-
      in-law—
God shield you mean it not, 'daughter' and 'mother'
So strive upon your pulse! What, pale again?
My fear hath catched your fondness! Now I see
The mystery of your loneliness, and find
Your salt tears' head. Now to all sense 'tis gross...
170 You love my son! invention is ashamed,
Against the proclamation of thy passion,
To say thou dost not: therefore tell me true—
But tell me then, 'tis so—for look, thy cheeks
Confess it, th'one to th'other, and thine eyes
See it so grossly shown in thy behaviours,
That in their kind they speak it—only sin
And hellish obstinacy tie thy tongue,
That truth should be suspected. Speak, is't so?
If it be so, you have wound a goodly clew;
180 If it be not, forswear't: howe'er, I charge thee,
As heaven shall work in me for thine avail,

To tell me truly.
  Helena [*kneels*].   Good madam, pardon me!
  Countess. Do you love my son?
  Helena.   Your pardon, noble mistress!
  Countess. Love you my son?
  Helena.   Do not you love him, madam?
  Countess. Go not about; my love hath in't a bond
Whereof the world takes note: come, come, disclose
The state of your affection, for your passions
Have to the full appeached.
  Helena.   Then, I confess,
Here on my knee, before high heaven and you,
That before you, and next unto high heaven,   190
I love your son...
My friends were poor but honest, so's my love:
Be not offended, for it hurts not him
That he is loved of me: I follow him not
By any token of presumptuous suit,
Nor would I have him till I do deserve him,
Yet never know how that desert should be...
I know I love in vain, strive against hope;
Yet, in this captious and inteemable sieve,
I still pour in the waters of my love,   200
And lack not to lose still: thus, Indian-like,
Religious in mine error, I adore
The sun, that looks upon his worshipper,
But knows of him no more....My dearest madam,
Let not your hate encounter with my love
For loving where you do: but if yourself,
Whose agéd honour cites a virtuous youth,
Did ever in so true a flame of liking
†Love chastely, and wish dearly that your Dian
Was both herself and Love, O, then give pity   210
To her, whose state is such, that cannot choose

But lend and give where she is sure to lose;
That seeks not to find that her search implies,
But, riddle-like, lives sweetly where she dies.
   Countess. Had you not lately an intent, speak truly,
To go to Paris?
   Helena.   Madam, I had.
   Countess.   Wherefore? tell true.
   Helena. I will tell truth, by grace itself, I swear...
You know my father left me some prescriptions
Of rare and proved effects, such as his reading
220 And manifest experience had collected
For general sovereignty; and that he willed me
In heedfull'st reservation to bestow them,
†As notes, whose faculties inclusive were,
More than they were in note: amongst the rest,
There is a remedy, approved, set down,
To cure the desperate languishings whereof
The king is rendered lost.
   Countess.   This was your motive
For Paris, was it? speak.
   Helena. My lord your son made me to think of this;
230 Else Paris, and the medicine, and the king,
Had from the conversation of my thoughts
Haply been absent then.
   Countess.   But think you, Helen,
If you should tender your supposéd aid,
He would receive it? He and his physicians
Are of a mind—he, that they cannot help him;
They, that they cannot help. How shall they credit
A poor unlearnéd virgin, when the schools,
Embowelled of their doctrine, have left off
The danger to itself?
   Helena.   †There's something hints,
240 More than my father's skill, which was the great'st

Of his profession, that his good receipt
Shall for my legacy be sanctified
By th' luckiest stars in heaven, and would
      your honour
But give me leave to try success, I'd venture
The well-lost life of mine on his grace's cure
By such a day and hour.
  Countess.   Dost thou believe't?
  Helena. Ay, madam, knowingly.
  Countess. Why, Helen, thou shalt have my leave
      and love,
Means and attendants, and my loving greetings
To those of mine in court. I'll stay at home   250
And pray God's blessing into thy attempt:
Be gone to-morrow, and be sure of this,
What I can help thee to, thou shalt not miss.   [*they go*

[2. 1.]   *A room in the King's palace at Paris;*
       at the back a closet with a couch

A flourish of cornets. 'Enter the KING' borne by attend-
ants in his chair 'with divers young lords taking leave
for the Florentine war'; among them BERTRAM and
PAROLLES

  King. Farewell, young lords! these warlike principles
Do not throw from you—and you, my lords farewell!
Share the advice betwixt you. If both gain all,
The gift doth stretch itself as 'tis received,
And is enough for both.
  1 *Lord.*   'Tis our hope, sir,
After, well-entered soldiers to return
And find your grace in health.
  King. No, no, it cannot be; and yet my heart
Will not confess he owes the malady

10 That doth my life besiege...Farewell, young lords!
Whether I live or die, be you the sons
Of worthy Frenchmen: let higher Italy
(Those bated that inherit but the fall
Of the last monarchy) see that you come
Not to woo honour, but to wed it. When
The bravest questant shrinks, find what you seek,
That fame may cry you loud...I say, farewell.

　　2 *Lord.*　Health, at your bidding, serve
　　　　your majesty!

　　King. Those girls of Italy, take heed of them.
20 They say, our French lack language to deny,
If they demand: beware of being captives,
Before you serve.

　　Both.　　　　　Our hearts receive your warnings.

　　King. Farewell. [*to attendants*] Come hither to me.
　　　　　　　[*he swoons and is carried to the couch,
　　　　　　　　before which curtains are drawn*

　　1 *Lord.* O my sweet lord, that you will stay
　　　　behind us!

　　Parolles. 'Tis not his fault, the spark.

　　2 *Lord.*　　　　　　　O, 'tis brave wars!

　　(*Parolles* [*shudders*]. Most admirable! I have seen
　　　　those wars.

　　Bertram. I am commanded here, and kept a
　　　　coil with

'Too young,' and 'the next year,' and ''tis too early.'

　　Parolles. An thy mind stand to't, boy, steal
　　　　away bravely.

30 *Bertram.* I shall stay here the forehorse to a smock,
Creaking my shoes on the plain masonry,
Till honour be bought up, and no sword worn
But one to dance with! By heaven, I'll steal away.

　　1 *Lord.* There's honour in the theft.

Parolles.   Commit it, count.

2 Lord. I am your accessary, and so farewell.

Bertram. I grow to you, and our parting is a tortured body.

1 Lord. Farewell, captain.

2 Lord. Sweet Monsieur Parolles!

Parolles. Noble heroes, my sword and yours are kin. 40
Good sparks and lustrous, a word, good metals: you
shall find in the regiment of the Spinii one Captain
Spurio, with his cicatrice, an emblem of war, here on
his sinister cheek; it was this very sword entrenched it:
say to him, I live, and observe his reports for me.

1 Lord. We shall, noble captain.

Parolles. Mars dote on you for his novices! [*the lords
go*] What will ye do?

> *At this, the curtains are drawn aside, discovering
> the King in his chair; attendants bear him forward*

Bertram [*finger on lip*]. Stay: the king!

Parolles [*hurries him away*]. Use a more spacious 50
ceremony to the noble lords, you have restrained yourself
within the list of too cold an adieu: be more expressive
to them; for they wear themselves in the cap of the time,
there do muster true gait, eat, speak, and move under
the influence of the most received star, and though the
devil lead the measure, such are to be followed; after
them, and take a more dilated farewell.

Bertram. And I will do so.

Parolles. Worthy fellows; and like to prove most
sinewy sword-men.   [*Bertram and Parolles go off* 60

> *The attendants set down the chair; LAFEU enters*

Lafeu [*kneels*]. Pardon, my lord, for me and for
    my tidings.

King. I'll fee thee to stand up.

Lafeu [*rises*]. Then here's a man stands that has
    brought his pardon.
I would you had kneeled, my lord, to ask me mercy,
And that at my bidding you could so stand up.
    King. I would I had, so I had broke thy pate
And asked thee mercy for't.
    Lafeu.   Good faith, across!
But, my good lord, 'tis thus—will you be cured
Of your infirmity?
    King.   No.
    Lafeu.   O, will you eat
70 No grapes, my royal fox? yes, but you will
My noble grapes, an if my royal fox
Could reach them: I have seen a medicine
That's able to breathe life into a stone,
Quicken a rock, and make you dance canary
With spritely fire and motion, whose simple touch
Is powerful to araise King Pepin, nay,
To give great Charlemain a pen in's hand,
And write to her a love-line.
    King.   What 'her' is this?
    Lafeu. Why, Doctor She: my lord, there's one arrived,
80 If you will see her: now, by my faith and honour,
If seriously I may convey my thoughts
In this my light deliverance, I have spoke
With one that, in her sex, her years, profession,
Wisdom and constancy, hath amazed me more
Than I dare blame my weakness: will you see her,
For that is her demand, and know her business?
That done, laugh well at me.
    King.   Now, good Lafeu,
Bring in the admiration, that we with thee
May spend our wonder too, or take off thine
By wond'ring how thou took'st it.

Lafeu.   Nay, I'll fit you,   90
And not be all day neither.   [*Lafeu hurries out*
King. Thus he his special nothing ever prologues.

    LAFEU *returns, holding open the door for one to*
                follow him

Lafeu. Nay, come your ways.

          HELENA *timidly enters*

King.   This haste hath wings indeed.
Lafeu. Nay, come your ways!
This is his majesty, say your mind to him.
A traitor you do look like, but such traitors
His majesty seldom fears. I am Cressid's uncle,
That dare leave two together. Fare you well. [*he goes*
   King. Now, fair one, does your business follow us?
Helena. Ay, my good lord.   100
Gerard de Narbon was my father;
In what he did profess, well-found.
   King.   I knew him.
Helena. The rather will I spare my praises
     towards him—
Knowing him is enough...On's bed of death
Many receipts he gave me, chiefly one,
Which as the dearest issue of his practice
And of his old experience th'only darling,
He bad me store up, as a triple eye,
Safer than mine own two, more dear; I have so:
And, hearing your high majesty is touched   110
With that malignant cause wherein the honour
Of my dear father's gift stands chief in power,
I come to tender it, and my appliance,
With all bound humbleness.
   King.   We thank you, maiden,
But may not be so credulous of cure,

When our most learnéd doctors leave us, and
The congregated College have concluded
That labouring art can never ransom nature
From her inaidible estate: I say we must not
120 So stain our judgement, or corrupt our hope,
To prostitute our past-cure malady
To empirics, or to dissever so
Our great self and our credit, to esteem
A senseless help, when help past sense we deem.

Helena. My duty then shall pay me for my pains:
I will no more enforce mine office on you;
Humbly entreating from your royal thoughts
A modest one, to bear me back again.

King. I cannot give thee less, to be called grateful...
130 Thou thought'st to help me, and such thanks I give
As one near death to those that wish him live:
But what at full I know, thou know'st no part,
I knowing all my peril, thou no art.

Helena. What I can do can do no hurt to try,
Since you set up your rest 'gainst remedy:
He that of greatest works is finisher,
Oft does them by the weakest minister:
So holy writ in babes hath judgement shown,
When judges have been babes; great floods have flown
140 From simple sources; and great seas have dried
When miracles have by the greatest been denied.
Oft expectation fails, and most oft there
Where most it promises; and oft it hits,
Where hope is coldest, and despair most fits.

King. I must not hear thee, fare thee well,
        kind maid.
Thy pains not used must by thyself be paid.
Proffers not took reap thanks for their reward.

Helena. Inspiréd merit so by breath is barred.

It is not so with Him that all things knows,
As 'tis with us that square our guess by shows: 150
But most it is presumption in us, when
The help of heaven we count the act of men.
Dear sir, to my endeavours give consent,
Of heaven, not me, make an experiment.
I am not an impostor, that proclaim
Myself against the level of mine aim,
But know I think, and think I know most sure,
My art is not past power, nor you past cure.
    King. Art thou so confident? Within what space
Hop'st thou my cure?
    Helena.   The great'st grace lending grace,   160
Ere twice the horses of the sun shall bring
Their fiery torcher his diurnal ring,
Ere twice in murk and occidental damp
Moist Hesperus hath quenched her sleepy lamp;
Or four and twenty times the pilot's glass
Hath told the thievish minutes how they pass;
What is infirm from your sound parts shall fly,
Health shall live free, and sickness freely die.
    King. Upon thy certainty and confidence,
What dar'st thou venture?
    Helena.   Tax of impudence,   170
A strumpet's boldness, a divulgéd shame,
Traduced by odious ballads; my maiden's name
Seared; otherwise—ne worse of worst—extended
With vilest torture let my life be ended.
    King. Methinks in thee some blesséd spirit doth speak
His powerful sound within an organ weak:
And what impossibility would slay
In common sense, sense saves another way...
Thy life is dear, for all that life can rate
Worth name of life in thee hath estimate;   180

†Youth, beauty, wisdom, courage, all
That happiness and prime can happy call:
Thou this to hazard needs must intimate
Skill infinite or monstrous desperate.
Sweet practiser, thy physic I will try,
That ministers thine own death if I die.
   Helena. If I break time, or flinch in property
Of what I spoke, unpitied let me die,
And well deserved: not helping, death's my fee,
190 But if I help what do you promise me?
    King. Make thy demand.
    Helena.   But will you make it even?
    King. Ay, by my sceptre and my hopes of heaven.
    Helena. Then shalt thou give me with thy
          kingly hand
What husband in thy power I will command:
Exempted be from me the arrogance
To choose from forth the royal blood of France,
My low and humble name to propagate
With any branch or image of thy state:
But such a one, thy vassal, whom I know
200 Is free for me to ask, thee to bestow.
   King. Here is my hand—the premises observed,
Thy will by my performance shall be served:
So make the choice of thy own time, for I,
Thy resolved patient, on thee still rely...
More should I question thee, and more I must,
Though more to know could not be more to trust;
From whence thou cam'st, how tended on—but rest
Unquestioned welcome, and undoubted blest.
Give me some help here, ho! If thou proceed
210 As high as word, my deed shall match thy deed.

    A flourish of trumpets; attendants carry him away

[2. 2.]   *A room in the palace of Rousillon*

COUNTESS *and* CLOWN

Countess. Come on, sir. I shall now put you to the height of your breeding.

Clown. I will show myself highly fed and lowly taught. I know my business is but to the court.

Countess. To the court! why, what place make you special, when you put off that with such contempt? 'But to the court!'

Clown. Truly, madam, if God have lent a man any manners, he may easily put it off at court: he that cannot make a leg, put off's cap, kiss his hand, and say nothing, 10 has neither leg, hands, lip, nor cap; and, indeed, such a fellow, to say precisely, were not for the court. But for me, I have an answer will serve all men.

Countess. Marry, that's a bountiful answer that fits all questions.

Clown. It is like a barber's chair that fits all buttocks—the pin-buttock, the quatch-buttock, the brawn-buttock, or any buttock.

Countess. Will your answer serve fit to all questions?

Clown. As fit as ten groats is for the hand of an 20 attorney, as your French crown for your taffety punk, as Tib's rush for Tom's forefinger, as a pancake for Shrove Tuesday, a morris for May-day, as the nail to his hole, the cuckold to his horn, as a scolding quean to a wrangling knave, as the nun's lip to the friar's mouth, nay, as the pudding to his skin.

Countess. Have you, I say, an answer of such fitness for all questions?

Clown. From below your duke to beneath your constable, it will fit any question.

Countess. It must be an answer of most monstrous size that must fit all demands.

Clown. But a trifle neither, in good faith, if the learned should speak truth of it: here it is, and all that belongs to't. Ask me if I am a courtier, it shall do you no harm to learn.

Countess. To be young again, if we could...I will be a fool in question, hoping to be the wiser by your answer. I pray you, sir, are you a courtier?

40 *Clown.* O Lord, sir!—There's a simple putting off: more, more, a hundred of them.

Countess. Sir, I am a poor friend of yours, that loves you.

Clown. O Lord, sir!—Thick! thick! spare not me.

Countess. I think, sir, you can eat none of this homely meat.

Clown. O Lord, sir!—Nay, put me to't, I warrant you.

Countess. You were lately whipped, sir, as I think.

Clown. O Lord, sir!—Spare not me.

Countess. Do you cry, 'O Lord, sir!' at your whipping,
50 and 'spare not me'? Indeed, your 'O Lord, sir!' is very sequent to your whipping; you would answer very well to a whipping, if you were but bound to't.

Clown. I ne'er had worse luck in my life in my 'O Lord, sir!' I see things may serve long, but not serve ever.

Countess. I play the noble housewife with the time, To entertain it so merrily with a fool.

Clown. O Lord, sir!—Why, there't serves well again.

Countess. An end, sir, to your business: give
      Helen this,
60 And urge her to a present answer back.
Commend me to my kinsmen and my son.
This is not much.

Clown. Not much commendation to them?

Countess. Not much employment for you. You understand me?

Clown. Most fruitfully. I am there before my legs.

Countess. Haste you again.

                              [*they go out by different doors*

[2. 3.] *A room in the King's palace at Paris;*
            at the back two chairs of state

BERTRAM, LAFEU, *and* PAROLLES

Lafeu. They say miracles are past, and we have our philosophical persons, to make modern and familiar, things supernatural and causeless. Hence is it that we make trifles of terrors, ensconcing ourselves into seeming knowledge, when we should submit ourselves to an unknown fear.

Parolles. Why, 'tis the rarest argument of wonder that hath shot out in our latter times.

Bertram. And so 'tis.

Lafeu. To be relinquished of the artists—   10

Parolles. So I say.

†*Lafeu.* Both of Galen and Paracelsus.

Parolles. So I say.

Lafeu. Of all the learned and authentic fellows—

Parolles. Right, so I say.

Lafeu. That gave him out incurable—

Parolles. Why, there 'tis, so say I too.

Lafeu. Not to be helped—

Parolles. Right, as 'twere a man assured of a—

Lafeu. Uncertain life, and sure death.   20

Parolles. Just, you say well: so would I have said.

Lafeu. I may truly say, it is a novelty to the world.

Parolles. It is, indeed: if you will have it in showing, you shall read it in †what-do-ye-call't there?

                                        3-2

Lafeu [*takes a ballad from his belt*]. 'A showing of a heavenly effect in an earthly actor.'

Parolles. That's it, I would have said the very same.

Lafeu. Why, your dolphin is not lustier: 'fore me I speak in respect—

30 *Parolles.* Nay, 'tis strange, 'tis very strange, that is the brief and the tedious of it, and he's of a most facinorous spirit that will not acknowledge it to be the—

Lafeu. Very hand of heaven.

Parolles. Ay, so I say.

Lafeu. In a most weak—

Parolles. And debile minister, great power, great transcendence, which should, indeed, give us a further use to be made than alone the recovery of the king, as 40 to be—

Lafeu. Generally thankful.

The KING *enters with* HELENA *and attendants*

Parolles. I would have said it. You say well... Here comes the king.

Lafeu. Lustick! as the Dutchman says: I'll like a maid the better, whilst I have a tooth in my head: why, he's able to lead her a coranto.

Parolles. Mort du vinaigre! Is not this Helen?

Lafeu. 'Fore God, I think so.

King. Go, call before me all the lords in court.

[*an attendant goes*

50 Sit, my preserver, by thy patient's side,

[*he leads her to the chairs of state*

And with this healthful hand, whose banished sense Thou hast repealed, a second time receive The confirmation of my promised gift, Which but attends thy naming....   [*they sit*

'*Enter three or four lords*'; *they stand before the
King,* BERTRAM *joining them*

Fair maid, send forth thine eye—this youthful parcel
Of noble bachelors stand at my bestowing,
O'er whom both sovereign power and father's voice
I have to use: thy frank election make,
Thou hast power to choose, and they none to forsake.
Helena. To each of you one fair and virtuous mistress 60
Fall, when Love please! marry, to each but one!
(*Lafeu* [*at a distance, to Parolles*]. I'd give bay Curtal
          and his furniture,
My mouth no more were broken than these boys',
And writ as little beard.
King.   Peruse them well:
Not one of those but had a noble father.
Helena [*rises*]. Gentlemen,
Heaven hath, through me, restored the king to health.
All. We understand it, and thank heaven for you.
Helena. I am a simple maid, and therein wealthiest
That I protest I simply am a maid...   70
Please it your majesty, I have done already:
The blushes in my cheeks thus whisper me,
'We blush that thou shouldst choose; but, be refused...
Let the white death sit on thy cheek for ever,
We'll ne'er come there again.'
King.   Make choice and see,
Who shuns thy love shuns all his love in me.
Helena. Now, Dian, from thy altar do I fly,
And to imperial Love, that god most high,
Do my sighs stream...['*she addresses her to a lord*'] Sir,
          will you hear my suit?
1 *Lord.* And grant it.
Helena.   Thanks, sir—all the rest is mute. 80
                                        [*he bows*

(*Lafeu.* I had rather be in this choice, than throw
ames-ace for my life.

Helena [*passes to another lord*]. The honour, sir, that
　　flames in your fair eyes,
Before I speak, too threat'ningly replies:
Love make your fortunes twenty times above
Her that so wishes and her humble love!

2 *Lord.* No better, if you please.

Helena. 　　　　　　　　My wish receive,
Which great Love grant! and so, I take my leave.

　　　　　　　　　　　　　　[*she passes on*

(*Lafeu.* Do all they deny her? An they were sons of
90 mine, I'd have them whipped, or I would send them
to th' Turk to make eunuchs of.

Helena [*to the third lord*]. Be not afraid that I your
　　hand should take,
I'll never do you wrong for your own sake:
Blessing upon your vows! and in your bed
Find fairer fortune, if you ever wed! 　　[*she passes on*

(*Lafeu.* These boys are boys of ice, they'll none have
her: sure, they are bastards to the English, the French
ne'er got 'em.

Helena [*to the fourth lord*]. You are too young, too
　　happy, and too good,
100 To make yourself a son out of my blood.

4 *Lord.* Fair one, I think not so. 　　[*she passes on*

(*Lafeu.* There's one grape yet—I am sure thy father
drunk wine—but if thou be'st not an ass, I am a youth
of fourteen; I have known thee already.

Helena [*to Bertram*]. I dare not say I take you, but I give
Me and my service, ever whilst I live,
Into your guiding power...This is the man.

King. Why then, young Bertram, take her, she's
　　thy wife.

Bertram. My wife, my liege? I shall beseech
    your highness,
In such a business give me leave to use   110
The help of mine own eyes.
King.   Know'st thou not, Bertram,
What she has done for me?
Bertram.   Yes, my good lord;
But never hope to know why I should marry her.
King. Thou know'st she has raised me from my
    sickly bed.
Bertram. But follows it, my lord, to bring me down
Must answer for your raising? I know her well;
She had her breeding at my father's charge:
A poor physician's daughter my wife! Disdain
Rather corrupt me ever!
King. 'Tis only title thou disdain'st in her,
    the which   120
I can build up...Strange is it, that our bloods,
Of colour, weight, and heat, poured all together,
Would quite confound distinction, yet stand off
In differences so mighty....If she be
All that is virtuous (save what thou dislik'st,
A poor physician's daughter) thou dislik'st
Of virtue for a name; but do not so:
From lowest place when virtuous things proceed,
The place is dignified by th'doer's deed:
Where great additions swell's, and virtue none,   130
It is a dropsied honour: good alone
Is good, without a name; vileness is so:
The property by what it is should go,
Not by the title....She is young, wise, fair;
In these to nature she's immediate heir;
And these breed honour: that is honour's scorn,
Which challenges itself as honour's born,

And is not like the sire: honours thrive,
When rather from our acts we them derive
140 Than our foregoers: the mere word's a slave,
Deboshed on every tomb, on every grave
A lying trophy, and as oft is dumb
Where dust and damned oblivion is the tomb
Of honoured bones indeed. What should be said?
If thou canst like this creature as a maid,
I can create the rest: virtue and she
Is her own dower; honour and wealth, from me.
 Bertram. I cannot love her, nor will strive to do't.
 King. Thou wrong'st thyself, if thou shouldst strive
  to choose.
150 *Helena.* That you are well restored, my lord,
  I'm glad;
Let the rest go.
 King. My honour's at the stake, which to defeat,
I must produce my power. [*rises*] Here, take
  her hand,
Proud scornful boy, unworthy this good gift,
That dost in vile misprision shackle up
My love and her desert; that canst not dream,
We, poising us in her defective scale,
Shall weigh thee to the beam: that wilt not know,
It is in us to plant thine honour where
160 We please to have it grow. Check thy contempt:
Obey our will, which travails in thy good:
Believe not thy disdain, but presently
Do thine own fortunes that obedient right
Which both thy duty owes and our power claims,
Or I will throw thee from my care for ever
Into the staggers and the careless lapse
Of youth and ignorance; both my revenge and hate,
Loosing upon thee in the name of justice,

Without all terms of pity. Speak, thine answer!

Bertram. Pardon, my gracious lord; for I submit   170
My fancy to your eyes. When I consider
What great creation and what dole of honour
Flies where you bid it, I find that she which late
Was in my nobler thoughts most base, is now
The praiséd of the king—who, so ennobled,
Is as 'twere born so.

King.   Take her by the hand,
And tell her she is thine: to whom I promise
A counterpoise; if not to thy estate,
A balance more replete.

Bertram.   I take her hand.

King. Good fortune and the favour of the king   180
Smile upon this contract; whose ceremony
Shall seem expedient on the now-born brief,
And be performed to-night: the solemn feast
Shall more attend upon the coming space,
Expecting absent friends. As thou lov'st her,
Thy love's to me religious; else, does err.

> [*all depart save Lafeu and Parolles who 'stay
> behind, commenting of this wedding'*

Lafeu. Do you hear, monsieur? a word with you.

Parolles. Your pleasure, sir?

Lafeu. Your lord and master did well to make his
recantation.   190

Parolles. Recantation! My lord! my master!

Lafeu. Ay; is it not a language I speak?

Parolles. A most harsh one, and not to be understood
without bloody succeeding. My master!

Lafeu. Are you companion to the Count Rousillon?

Parolles. To any count, to all counts: to what is man!

Lafeu. To what is count's man: count's master is of
another style.

Parolles. You are too old, sir; let it satisfy you, you
200 are too old.

Lafeu. I must tell thee, sirrah, I write man; to which
title age cannot bring thee.

Parolles [*his hand upon his sword*]. What I dare too
well do, I dare not do.

Lafeu. I did think thee, for two ordinaries, to be a
pretty wise fellow; thou didst make tolerable vent of
thy travel—it might pass: yet the scarfs and the ban-
nerets about thee did manifoldly dissuade me from
believing thee a vessel of too great a burden. I have now
210 found thee—when I lose thee again, I care not: yet art
thou good for nothing but taking up, and that thou'rt
scarce worth.

Parolles. Hadst thou not the privilege of antiquity
upon thee,—

Lafeu. Do not plunge thyself too far in anger, lest
thou hasten thy trial; which if—Lord have mercy on
thee for a hen! So, my good window of lattice, fare thee
well, thy casement I need not open, for I look through
thee....Give me thy hand.

220 *Parolles* [*does so*]. My lord, you give me most egregious
indignity.

Lafeu [*shakes his hand*]. Ay, with all my heart, and
thou art worthy of it.

Parolles. I have not, my lord, deserved it.

Lafeu. Yes, good faith, every dram of it, and I will
not bate thee a scruple.

Parolles. Well, I shall be wiser.

Lafeu. E'en as soon as thou canst, for thou hast to pull
at a smack o'th' contrary. If ever thou be'st bound in
230 thy scarf and beaten, thou shalt find what it is to be
proud of thy bondage. I have a desire to hold my
acquaintance with thee, or rather my knowledge, that
I may say, in the default, he is a man I know.

Parolles. My lord, you do me most insupportable vexation.

Lafeu. I would it were hell-pains for thy sake, and my poor doing eternal: for doing I am past, as I will by thee, in what motion age will give me leave.

                    [*he passes him swiftly and goes out*

Parolles. Well, thou hast a son shall take this disgrace off me; scurvy, old, filthy, scurvy lord! Well, I must be 240 patient, there is no fettering of authority. I'll beat him, by my life, if I can meet him with any convenience, an he were double and double a lord. I'll have no more pity of his age than I would have of—I'll beat him, an if I could but meet him again.

LAFEU *returns*

Lafeu. Sirrah, your lord and master's married, there's news for you; you have a new mistress.

Parolles. I most unfeignedly beseech your lordship to make some reservation of your wrongs. He is my good lord—whom I serve above, is my master.   250

Lafeu. Who? God?

Parolles. Ay, sir.

Lafeu. The devil it is that's thy master. Why dost thou garter up thy arms o' this fashion? dost make hose of thy sleeves? do other servants so? Thou wert best set thy lower part where thy nose stands. By mine honour, if I were but two hours younger, I'd beat thee: me-think'st thou art a general offence, and every man should beat thee: I think thou wast created for men to breathe themselves upon thee.   260

Parolles. This is hard and undeserved measure, my lord.

Lafeu. Go to, sir, you were beaten in Italy for picking a kernel out of a pomegranate, you are a vagabond and

no true traveller; you are more saucy with lords and
honourable personages than the commission of your
birth and virtue gives you heraldry. You are not worth
another word else I'd call you knave. I leave you.

[*he goes*

Parolles. Good, very good, it is so then: good, very
270 good, let it be concealed awhile.

BERTRAM *enters*

(*Bertram.* Undone, and forfeited to cares for ever!
Parolles. What's the matter, sweet-heart?
(*Bertram.* Although before the solemn priest
        I have sworn,
I will not bed her.
Parolles. What, what, sweet-heart?
Bertram. O my Parolles, they have married me:
I'll to the Tuscan wars, and never bed her.
Parolles. France is a dog-hole, and it no more merits
The tread of a man's foot: to th' wars!
280 *Bertram.* There's letters from my mother: what
        th'import is,
I know not yet.
Parolles. Ay, that would be known...To th' wars,
        my boy, to th' wars!
He wears his honour in a box unseen,
That hugs his kicky-wicky here at home,
Spending his manly marrow in her arms,
Which should sustain the bound and high curvet
Of Mars's fiery steed...To other regions!
France is a stable, we that dwell in't jades,
Therefore to th' war!
290 *Bertram.* It shall be so. I'll send her to my house,
Acquaint my mother with my hate to her,
And wherefore I am fled; write to the king

That which I durst not speak: his present gift
Shall furnish me to those Italian fields,
Where noble fellows strike: war is no strife
To the dark house and the detested wife.
　Parolles. Will this capriccio hold in thee, art sure?
　Bertram. Go with me to my chamber, and
　　advise me.
I'll send her straight away: to-morrow
I'll to the wars, she to her single sorrow.　　　　　　300
　Parolles. Why, these balls bound, there's noise in
　　it. 'Tis hard;
A young man married is a man that's marred:
Therefore away, and leave her bravely; go.
The king has done you wrong; but, hush, 'tis so.

　　　　　　　　　　　　　　　　　　　[they go

[2. 4.]　　*Another room in the King's palace*

'*Enter HELENA and CLOWN*'

　Helena. My mother greets me kindly. Is she well?
　Clown. She is not well, but yet she has her health, she's
very merry, but yet she is not well: but thanks be given,
she's very well and wants nothing i'th' world; but yet
she is not well.
　Helena. If she be very well, what does she ail, that
she's not very well?
　Clown. Truly, she's very well indeed, but for two
things.
　Helena. What two things?　　　　　　　　　　　　10
　Clown. One, that she's not in heaven, whither God
send her quickly: the other, that she's in earth, from
whence God send her quickly.

Parolles. Bless you, my fortunate lady!

Helena. I hope, sir, I have your good will to have mine own good fortunes.

Parolles. You had my prayers to lead them on, and to keep them on have them still. O, my knave, how does my old lady?

20 *Clown.* So that you had her wrinkles, and I her money, I would she did as you say.

Parolles. Why, I say nothing.

Clown. Marry, you are the wiser man; for many a man's tongue shakes out his master's undoing: to say nothing, to do nothing, to know nothing, and to have nothing, is to be a great part of your title—which is within a very little of nothing.

Parolles. Away, th'art a knave.

Clown. You should have said, sir, 'before a knave 30 th'art a knave,' that's, before me th'art a knave: this had been truth, sir.

Parolles. Go to, thou art a witty fool, I have found thee.

Clown. Did you find me in yourself, sir? or were you taught to find me?

†*Parolles.* In myself.

Clown. The search, sir, was profitable; and much fool may you find in you, even to the world's pleasure and the increase of laughter.

Parolles. A good knave, i' faith, and well fed.
40 Madam, my lord will go away to-night,
A very serious business calls on him:
The great prerogative and rite of love,
Which as your due time claims, he does acknowledge,
But puts it off to a compelled restraint;
Whose want, and whose delay, is strewed with sweets,
Which they distil now in the curbéd time,

To make the coming hour o'erflow with joy,
And pleasure drown the brim.

Helena. What's his will else?

Parolles. That you will take your instant leave
  o'th' king,
And make this haste as your own good proceeding, 50
Strengthened with what apology you think
May make it probable need.

Helena. What more commands he?

Parolles. That, having this obtained, you presently
Attend his further pleasure.

Helena. In every thing I wait upon his will.

Parolles. I shall report it so. [*goes*

Helena. I pray you.—Come, sirrah.
[*they go*

[2. 5.] *Another room in the same*
'*Enter* LAFEU *and* BERTRAM'

Lafeu. But I hope your lordship thinks not him a
soldier.

Bertram. Yes, my lord, and of very valiant approof.

Lafeu. You have it from his own deliverance.

Bertram. And by other warranted testimony.

Lafeu. Then my dial goes not true, I took this lark
for a bunting.

Bertram. I do assure you, my lord, he is very great in
knowledge, and accordingly valiant.

Lafeu. I have then sinned against his experience and 10
transgressed against his valour, and my state that way
is dangerous, since I cannot yet find in my heart to
repent...

Enter PAROLLES

Here he comes, I pray you make us friends, I will
pursue the amity.

Parolles [*to Bertram*]. These things shall be done, sir.

Lafeu. Pray you, sir, who's his tailor?

Parolles. Sir?

Lafeu. O, I know him well. Ay sir, he, sir, 's a good
20 workman, a very good tailor.

(*Bertram.* Is she gone to the king?

(*Parolles.* She is.

(*Bertram.* Will she away to-night?

(*Parolles.* As you'll have her.

(*Bertram.* I have writ my letters, casketed my treasure,
Given order for our horses—and to-night,
When I should take possession of the bride,
End ere I do begin.

Lafeu. A good traveller is something at the latter end
30 of a dinner, but one that lies three thirds and uses a
known truth to pass a thousand nothings with, should
be once heard and thrice beaten....[*they turn to him*]
God save you, captain.

Bertram. Is there any unkindness between my lord
and you, monsieur?

Parolles. I know not how I have deserved to run into
my lord's displeasure.

Lafeu. You have made shift to run into't, boots and
spurs and all, like him that leaped into the custard; and
40 out of it you'll run again, rather than suffer question for
your residence.

Bertram. It may be you have mistaken him, my lord.

Lafeu. And shall do so ever, though I took him at's
prayers. Fare you well, my lord, and believe this of
me, there can be no kernel in this light nut; the soul of
this man is his clothes: trust him not in matter of heavy
consequence; I have kept of them tame and know their
natures....Farewell, monsieur, I have spoken better of
you than you have or will to deserve at my hand, but
50 we must do good against evil.   [*he goes*

Parolles. An idle lord, I swear.

Bertram [*hesitates*]. I think so.

Parolles. Why, do you not know him?

Bertram. Yes, I do know him well, and
    common speech

Gives him a worthy pass....

HELENA enters

                        Here comes my clog.

Helena. I have, sir, as I was commanded from you,
Spoke with the king, and have procured his leave
For present parting—only he desires
Some private speech with you.

Bertram.   I shall obey his will.

You must not marvel, Helen, at my course,   60
Which holds not colour with the time, nor does
The ministration and requiréd office
On my particular. Prepared I was not
For such a business, therefore am I found
So much unsettled...This drives me to entreat you
That presently you take your way for home,
And rather muse than ask why I entreat you,
For my respects are better than they seem,
And my appointments have in them a need
Greater than shows itself at the first view   70
To you that know them not....[*gives a letter*] This to
    my mother.

'Twill be two days ere I shall see you, so
I leave you to your wisdom.

Helena.   Sir, I can nothing say,
But that I am your most obedient servant.

Bertram. Come, come, no more of that.

Helena.   And ever shall
With true observance seek to eke out that

Wherein toward me my homely stars have failed
To equal my great fortune.
   Bertram.   Let that go:
My haste is very great. Farewell; hie home.
80 *Helena.* Pray, sir, your pardon.
   Bertram.   Well, what would you say?
   Helena. I am not worthy of the wealth I owe,
Nor dare I say 'tis mine...and yet it is—
But like a timorous thief most fain would steal
What law does vouch mine own.
   Bertram.   What would you have?
   Helena. Something, and scarce so much:
      nothing, indeed.
I would not tell you what I would, my lord...
Faith, yes—
Strangers and foes do sunder, and not kiss.
   Bertram. I pray you stay not, but in haste to horse.
90 *Helena.* I shall not break your bidding, good
      my lord...
   Bertram. Where are my other men, monsieur?—
      Farewell.   *[Helena departs*
Go thou toward home, where I will never come,
Whilst I can shake my sword, or hear the drum...
Away, and for our flight.
   Parolles.   Bravely, coragio!   *[they go*

[3. 1.]   *Florence. Before the Duke's palace*

'*Flourish. Enter the* DUKE OF FLORENCE, *the two
Frenchmen with a troop of soldiers*'

Duke. So that from point to point now have
      you heard
The fundamental reasons of this war;
Whose great decision hath much blood let forth,

And more thirsts after.

1 *Lord*.   Holy seems the quarrel
Upon your grace's part; black and fearful
On the opposer.

Duke. Therefore we marvel much our cousin France
Would in so just a business shut his bosom
Against our borrowing prayers.

2 *Lord*.   Good my lord,
The reasons of our state I cannot yield,   10
But like a common and an outward man,
That the great figure of a council frames
By self-unable motion—therefore dare not
Say what I think of it, since I have found
Myself in my incertain grounds to fail
As often as I guessed.

Duke.   Be it his pleasure.

1 *Lord*. But I am sure the younger of our nature,
That surfeit on their ease, will day by day
Come here for physic.

Duke.   Welcome shall they be:
And all the honours that can fly from us   20
Shall on them settle...You know your places well;
When better fall, for your avails they fell:
To-morrow to th' field!   [*a flourish; they pass on*

[3. 2.]   *A room in the palace of Rousillon*

The COUNTESS (*with a letter in her hand*) *and
the* CLOWN

Countess. It hath happened all as I would have had
it, save that he comes not along with her.

Clown. By my troth, I take my young lord to be a
very melancholy man.

Countess. By what observance, I pray you?

4-2

Clown. Why, he will look upon his boot and sing, mend the ruff and sing, ask questions and sing, pick his teeth and sing: I know a man that had this trick of melancholy sold a goodly manor for a song.

10 *Countess.* Let me see what he writes, and when he means to come.   [*she opens the letter*

(*Clown.* I have no mind to Isbel, since I was at court. Our old ling and our Isbels o'the country are nothing like your old ling and your Isbels o'the court: the brains of my Cupid's knocked out, and I begin to love, as an old man loves money, with no stomach.

Countess. What have we here?

Clown. E'en that you have there.   [*he goes*

Countess [*reads*]. 'I have sent you a daughter-in-law.
20 She hath recovered the king, and undone me: I have wedded her, not bedded her, and sworn to make the 'not' eternal. You shall hear I am run away, know it before the report come. If there be breadth enough in the world, I will hold a long distance. My duty to you.

                    Your unfortunate son,
                              BERTRAM.'

This is not well, rash and unbridled boy,
To fly the favours of so good a king,
To pluck his indignation on thy head,
30 By the misprising of a maid too virtuous
For the contempt of empire.

                    The CLOWN *returns*

Clown. O madam, yonder is heavy news within between two soldiers and my young lady.

Countess. What is the matter?

Clown. Nay, there is some comfort in the news, some comfort—your son will not be killed so soon as I thought he would.

Countess. Why should he be killed?

Clown. So say I, madam, if he run away, as I hear
he does. The danger is in standing to't, that's the loss 40
of men, though it be the getting of children. Here they
come will tell you more. For my part, I only hear your
son was run away.

HELENA enters with two gentlemen

1 *Gentleman.* Save you, good madam.

Helena. Madam, my lord is gone, for ever gone.

                              [*she sobs*

2 *Gentleman.* Do not say so.

Countess [*takes her in her arms*]. Think upon patience.
      Pray you, gentlemen,
I have felt so many quirks of joy and grief,
That the first face of neither, on the start,
Can woman me unto't...Where is my son, I
      pray you?   50

2 *Gentleman.* Madam, he's gone to serve the Duke
      of Florence.
We met him thitherward, for thence we came:
And after some dispatch in hand at court
Thither we bend again.

Helena. Look on his letter, madam, here's
      my passport.
[*reads*] 'When thou canst get the ring upon my
finger, which never shall come off, and show me a child
begotten of thy body that I am father to, then call me
husband: but in such a 'then' I write a 'never'.'
This is a dreadful sentence.   60

Countess. Brought you this letter, gentlemen?

1 *Gentleman.*   Ay, madam,
And for the contents' sake are sorry for our pains.

Countess. I prithee lady have a better cheer,

If thou engrossest all the griefs are thine,
Thou robb'st me of a moiety...He was my son,
But I do wash his name out of my blood,
And thou art all my child....Towards Florence is he?

  2 Gentleman. Ay, madam.

  Countess.   And to be a soldier?

  2 Gentleman. Such is his noble purpose,
    and, believe't,

70 The duke will lay upon him all the honour
That good convenience claims.

  Countess.   Return you thither?

  1 Gentleman. Ay, madam, with the swiftest wing
    of speed.

  Helena [*reads*]. 'Till I have no wife, I have nothing
    in France.'
'Tis bitter.

  Countess.   Find you that there?

  Helena.   Ay, madam.

  1 Gentleman. 'Tis but the boldness of his hand, haply,
which his heart was not consenting to.

  Countess. Nothing in France, until he have no wife!
There's nothing here that is too good for him
But only she, and she deserves a lord

80 That twenty such rude boys might tend upon
And call her hourly mistress. Who was with him?

  1 Gentleman. A servant only, and a gentleman
Which I have sometime known.

  Countess.   Parolles, was it not?

  1 Gentleman. Ay, my good lady, he.

  Countess. A very tainted fellow, and full of
    wickedness.
My son corrupts a well-derivéd nature
With his inducement.

  1 Gentleman.   Indeed, good lady,

The fellow has a deal of that too much,
Which holds him much to have.

Countess. Y'are welcome, gentlemen.   90
I will entreat you, when you see my son,
To tell him that his sword can never win
The honour that he loses: more I'll entreat you
Written to bear along.

2 *Gentleman.*   We serve you, madam,
In that and all your worthiest affairs.

Countess. Not so, but as we change our courtesies.
Will you draw near?

> [*the Countess goes out with the gentlemen;*
> *the Clown follows*

Helena. 'Till I have no wife, I have nothing
    in France.'
Nothing in France, until he has no wife!
Thou shalt have none, Rousillon, none in France,   100
Then hast thou all again....Poor lord! is't I
That chase thee from thy country and expose
Those tender limbs of thine to the event
Of the nonc-sparing war? and is it I
That drive thee from the sportive court, where thou
Wast shot at with fair eyes, to be the mark
Of smoky muskets? O you leaden messengers,
That ride upon the violent speed of fire,
†Fly with false aim, move the still-piecing air
That sings with piercing, do not touch my lord!   110
Whoever shoots at him, I set him there.
Whoever charges on his forward breast, •
I am the caitiff that do hold him to't.
And, though I kill him not, I am the cause
His death was so effected: better 'twere
I met the ravin lion when he roared
With sharp constraint of hunger: better 'twere

That all the miseries which nature owes
Were mine at once. No, come thou home, Rousillon,
120 Whence honour but of danger wins a scar,
As oft it loses all....I will be gone:
My being here it is that holds thee hence—
Shall I stay here to do't? no, no, although
The air of paradise did fan the house,
And angels officed all: I will be gone,
That pitiful rumour may report my flight,
To consolate thine ear. Come night! end day!
For with the dark, poor thief, I'll steal away. [*she goes*

[3. 3.]   *Florence. Before the Duke's palace*

Flourish. Enter the DUKE OF FLORENCE, BERTRAM,
   PAROLLES, *officers, soldiers, drum and trumpets*

Duke. The general of our horse thou art, and we,
Great in our hope, lay our best love and credence
Upon thy promising fortune.
   Bertram.   Sir, it is
A charge too heavy for my strength, but yet
We'll strive to bear it for your worthy sake
To th'extreme edge of hazard.
   Duke.   Then go thou forth,
And fortune play upon thy prosperous helm,
As thy auspicious mistress!
   Bertram.   This very day,
Great Mars, I put myself into thy file!
10 Make me but like my thoughts, and I shall prove
A lover of thy drum, hater of love.   [*they march off*

[3. 4.]   *A room in the palace of Rousillon*

COUNTESS *and* STEWARD

Countess. Alas! and would you take the letter of her?
Might you not know she would do as she has done,
By sending me a letter? Read it again.
  Steward [*reads*]. 'I am S. Jaques' pilgrim,
        thither gone:
  Ambitious love hath so in me offended,
That barefoot plod I the cold ground upon,
  With sainted vow my faults to have amended.
Write, write, that from the bloody course of war
  My dearest master, your dear son, may hie:
Bless him at home in peace, whilst I from far   10
  His name with zealous fervour sanctify:
His taken labours bid him me forgive;
  I, his despiteful Juno, sent him forth
From courtly friends with camping foes to live,
  Where death and danger dogs the heels of worth.
He is too good and fair for death and me,
Whom I myself embrace to set him free.'
  Countess. Ah, what sharp stings are in her
        mildest words!
Rinaldo, you did never lack advice so much,
As letting her pass so: had I spoke with her,   20
I could have well diverted her intents,
Which thus she hath prevented.
  Steward.   Pardon me, madam.
If I had given you this at over-night,
She might have been o'erta'en: and yet she writes,
Pursuit would be but vain.
  Countess.   What angel shall

Bless this unworthy husband? he cannot thrive,
Unless her prayers, whom heaven delights to hear
And loves to grant, reprieve him from the wrath
Of greatest justice....Write, write, Rinaldo,
30 To this unworthy husband of his wife,
Let every word weigh heavy of her worth
That he does weigh too light: my greatest grief,
Though little he do feel it, set down sharply.
Dispatch the most convenient messenger.
When haply he shall hear that she is gone,
He will return, and hope I may that she,
Hearing so much, will speed her foot again,
Led hither by pure love: which of them both
Is dearest to me, I have no skill in sense
40 To make distinction...Provide this messenger...
My heart is heavy and mine age is weak,
Grief would have tears, and sorrow bids me speak.

            [they go

[3. 5.]   *Without the walls of Florence*

Enter an old WIDOW *of Florence, her daughter* DIANA,
and MARIANA, *with other citizens; 'a tucket afar
off'*

Widow. Nay come, for if they do approach the city,
we shall lose all the sight.

Diana. They say the French count has done most
honourable service.

Widow. It is reported that he has taken their great'st
commander, and that with his own hand he slew the
duke's brother...[*tucket*] We have lost our labour, they
are gone a contrary way—hark! you may know by their
trumpets.

10 *Mariana.* Come, let's return again, and suffice our-

selves with the report of it....[*they turn*] Well, Diana,
take heed of this French earl. The honour of a maid is
her name, and no legacy is so rich as honesty.

Widow. I have told my neighbour how you have
been solicited by a gentleman his companion.

Mariana. I know that knave, hang him! one Parolles,
a filthy officer he is in those suggestions for the young
earl. Beware of them, Diana: their promises, entice-
ments, oaths, tokens, and all these engines of lust, are
not the things they go under: many a maid hath been 20
seduced by them. And the misery is, example, that so
terrible shows in the wrack of maidenhood, cannot for
all that dissuade succession, but that they are limed with
the twigs that threaten them. I hope I need not to
advise you further, but I hope your own grace will keep
you where you are, though there were no further danger
known but the modesty which is so lost.

Diana. You shall not need to fear me.

HELENA approaches disguised as a pilgrim

Widow. I hope so...Look, here comes a pilgrim, I
know she will lie at my house, thither they send one 30
another. I'll question her.
God save you, pilgrim! whither are you bound?

Helena. To S. Jaques le Grand.
Where do the palmers lodge, I do beseech you?

Widow. At the S. Francis here, beside the port.

Helena. Is this the way?

Widow. Ay, marry, is't....['*a march afar*'] Hark
    you! they come this way.
If you will tarry, holy pilgrim,
But till the troops come by,
I will conduct you where you shall be lodged,   40
The rather for I think I know your hostess?

As ample as myself.

Helena.   Is it yourself?

Widow. If you shall please so, pilgrim.

Helena. I thank you, and will stay upon your leisure.

Widow. You came, I think, from France?

Helena.   I did so.

Widow. Here you shall see a countryman of yours,
That has done worthy service.

Helena.   His name, I pray you.

Diana. The Count Rousillon: know you such a one?

Helena. But by the ear, that hears most nobly of him:

50 His face I know not.

Diana.   Whatsome'er he is,
He's bravely taken here. He stole from France,
As 'tis reported, for the king had married him
Against his liking. Think you it is so?

Helena. Ay, surely, the mere truth. I know
        his lady.

Diana. There is a gentleman that serves the count
Reports but coarsely of her.

Helena.   What's his name?

Diana. Monsieur Parolles.

Helena.   O, I believe with him,
In argument of praise, or to the worth
Of the great count himself, she is too mean

60 To have her name repeated—all her deserving
Is a reservéd honesty, and that
I have not heard examined.

Diana.   Alas, poor lady!
'Tis a hard bondage to become the wife
Of a detesting lord.

Widow. I warrant, good creature, wheresoe'er she is,
Her heart weighs sadly: this young maid might
        do her

A shrewd turn, if she pleased.
Helena.   How do you mean?
May be the amorous count solicits her
In the unlawful purpose.
Widow.   He does indeed,
And brokes with all that can in such a suit   70
Corrupt the tender honour of a maid:
But she is armed for him, and keeps her guard
In honestest defence.
Mariana. The gods forbid else!
Widow.   So, now they come...

*The Florentine army draws near with colours flying and
drums beating; BERTRAM and PAROLLES in the fore-
most ranks*

That is Antonio, the duke's eldest son,
That, Escalus.
Helena.   Which is the Frenchman?
Diana [*points*].   He—
That with the plume—'tis a most gallant fellow.
I would he loved his wife: if he were honester
He were much goodlier. Is't not a handsome
          gentleman?
Helena. I like him well.   80
Diana. 'Tis pity he is not honest: yond's that
          same knave
That leads him to these places: were I his lady,
I would poison that vile rascal.
Helena.   Which is he?
Diana. That jack-an-apes with scarfs. Why is he
          melancholy?
Helena. Perchance he's hurt i'th' battle.
Parolles [*mutters*]. Lose our drum! well.

Mariana. He's shrewdly vexed at something. Look,
he has spied us.   [*Parolles doffs his hat*
Widow. Marry, hang you!
90 *Mariana.* And your curtsy, for a ring-carrier!
                                        [*the soldiers pass on*
Widow. The troop is past...Come, pilgrim, I will
     bring you
Where you shall host: of enjoined penitents
There's four or five, to great S. Jaques bound,
Already at my house.
Helena.   I humbly thank you:
Please it this matron and this gentle maid
To eat with us to-night, the charge and thanking
Shall be for me; and, to requite you further,
I will bestow some precepts of this virgin
Worthy the note.
Both.   We'll take your offer kindly.
                              [*they walk towards the city*

[3. 6.]   *The camp before Florence*

BERTRAM *and the two French Lords approach*

2 *Lord.* Nay, good my lord, put him to't; let him
have his way.

1 *Lord.* If your lordship find him not a hilding, hold
me no more in your respect.

2 *Lord.* On my life, my lord, a bubble.

Bertram. Do you think I am so far deceived in him?

2 *Lord.* Believe it, my lord, in mine own direct
knowledge, without any malice, but to speak of him as
my kinsman, he's a most notable coward, an infinite
10 and endless liar, an hourly promise-breaker, the owner
of no one good quality worthy your lordship's entertainment.

1 *Lord.* It were fit you knew him, lest reposing too far in his virtue which he hath not, he might at some great and trusty business in a main danger fail you.

Bertram. I would I knew in what particular action to try him.

1 *Lord.* None better than to let him fetch off his drum, which you hear him so confidently undertake to do.

2 *Lord.* I, with a troop of Florentines, will suddenly 20 surprise him; such I will have, whom I am sure he knows not from the enemy: we will bind and hood-wink him so, that he shall suppose no other but that he is carried into the leaguer of the adversaries, when we bring him to our own tents...Be but your lordship present at his examination—if he do not, for the promise of his life and in the highest compulsion of base fear, offer to betray you and deliver all the intelligence in his power against you, and that with the divine forfeit of his soul upon oath, never trust my judgement in any thing.   30

1 *Lord.* O, for the love of laughter, let him fetch his drum. He says he has a stratagem for't: when your lordship sees the bottom of his success in't, and to what metal this counterfeit lump of ore will be melted, if you give him not John Drum's entertainment, your in-clining cannot be removed. Here he comes.

PAROLLES draws near, affecting melancholy

(2 *Lord.* O, for the love of laughter, hinder not the honour of his design, let him fetch off his drum in any hand.

Bertram. How now, monsieur! this drum sticks sorely 40 in your disposition.

1 *Lord.* A pox on't, let it go, 'tis but a drum.

Parolles. 'But a drum!' is't 'but a drum'? A drum so lost! There was excellent command—to charge in

with our horse upon our own wings, and to rend our
own soldiers!

1 *Lord*. That was not to be blamed in the command
of the service: it was a disaster of war that Cæsar himself
could not have prevented, if he had been there to
50 command.

Bertram. Well, we cannot greatly condemn our
success: some dishonour we had in the loss of that drum:
but it is not to be recovered.

Parolles. It might have been recovered.

Bertram. It might, but it is not now.

Parolles. It is to be recovered. But that the merit of
service is seldom attributed to the true and exact per-
former, I would have that drum or another, or 'hic
jacet.'

60 *Bertram*. Why, if you have a stomach, to't monsieur:
if you think your mystery in stratagem can bring this
instrument of honour again into his native quarter, be
magnanimous in the enterprise, and go on—I will grace
the attempt for a worthy exploit: if you speed well in
it, the duke shall both speak of it, and extend to you
what further becomes his greatness, even to the utmost
syllable of your worthiness.

Parolles. By the hand of a soldier, I will undertake
it.

70 *Bertram*. But you must not now slumber in it.

Parolles. I'll about it this evening, and I will presently
pen down my dilemmas, encourage myself in my
certainty, put myself into my mortal preparation; and
by midnight look to hear further from me.

Bertram. May I be bold to acquaint his grace you
are gone about it?

Parolles. I know not what the success will be, my
lord, but the attempt I vow.

Bertram. I know, th'art valiant—and, to the possibility
of thy soldiership, will subscribe for thee...Farewell.   80
Parolles. I love not many words.   [*he goes*
2 *Lord.* No more than a fish loves water....Is not this
a strange fellow, my lord, that so confidently seems to
undertake this business—which he knows is not to be
done—damns himself to do, and dares better be damned
than to do't.
1 *Lord.* Ycu do not know him, my lord, as we do.
Certain it is, that he will steal himself into a man's
favour and for a week escape a great deal of discoveries,
but when you find him out you have him ever after.   90
Bertram. Why, do you think he will make no deed at
all of this that so seriously he does address himself unto?
2 *Lord.* None in the world, but return with an invention, and clap upon you two or three probable lies:
but we have almost embossed him, you shall see his fall
to-night; for indeed he is not for your lordship's respect.
1 *Lord.* We'll make you some sport with the fox ere
we case him. He was first smoked by the old lord Lafeu.
When his disguise and he is parted, tell me what a sprat
you shall find him, which you shall see this very night. 100
2 *Lord.* I must go look my twigs, he shall be caught.
Bertram. Your brother, he shall go along with me.
2 *Lord.* As't please your lordship: I'll leave you.
    [*he goes*
Bertram. Now will I lead you to the house, and
    show you
The lass I spoke of.
1 *Lord.*   But you say she's honest.
Bertram. That's all the fault: I spoke with her
    but once,
And found her wondrous cold, but I sent to her,
By this same coxcomb that we have i'th' wind,

5   PSAW

Tokens and letters which she did re-send,
110 And this is all I have done...She's a fair creature,
Will you go see her?
 1 *Lord.*   With all my heart, my lord.
            [they walk away

 [3. 7.] *A room in the Widow's house at Florence*

    Enter HELENA *and* WIDOW

 Helena. If you misdoubt me that I am not she,
I know not how I shall assure you further,
But I shall lose the grounds I work upon.
 Widow. Though my estate be fall'n, I was well born,
Nothing acquainted with these businesses,
And would not put my reputation now
In any staining act.
 Helena.   Nor would I wish you.
First give me trust the count he is my husband,
And what to your sworn counsel I have spoken
10 Is so from word to word; and then you cannot,
By the good aid that I of you shall borrow,
Err in bestowing it.
 Widow.   I should believe you,
For you have showed me that which well approves
Y'are great in fortune.
 Helena.   Take this purse of gold,
And let me buy your friendly help thus far,
Which I will over-pay and pay again
When I have found it....[*she gives it*] The count he
  wooes your daughter,
Lays down his wanton siege before her beauty,
Resolved to carry her: let her in fine consent,
20 As we'll direct her how 'tis best to bear it:
Now his important blood will nought deny

That she'll demand: a ring the county wears,
That downward hath succeeded in his house
From son to son, some four or five descents
Since the first father wore it: this ring he holds
In most rich choice; yet in his idle fire,
To buy his will, it would not seem too dear,
Howe'er repented after.

Widow. Now I see
The bottom of your purpose.

Helena. You see it lawful then. It is no more 30
But that your daughter, ere she seems as won,
Desires this ring; appoints him an encounter;
In fine, delivers me to fill the time,
Herself most chastely absent: after this,
To marry her, I'll add three thousand crowns
To what is past already.

Widow. I have yielded:
Instruct my daughter how she shall persever,
That time and place with this deceit so lawful
May prove coherent. Every night he comes
With musics of all sorts and songs composed 40
To her unworthiness: it nothing steads us
To chide him from our eaves, for he persists
As if his life lay on't.

Helena. Why then to-night
Let us assay our plot, which if it speed,
Is wicked meaning in a lawful deed,
And lawful meaning in a lawful act,
Where both not sin, and yet a sinful fact:
But let's about it. [*they go*

[4. 1.]   *A field near the Florentine camp*

The second French Lord, 'with five or six other soldiers,
in ambush'; one bearing a drum

2 *Lord.* He can come no other way but by this
hedge-corner...When you sally upon him, speak what
terrible language you will: though you understand it
not yourselves, no matter: for we must not seem to
understand him, unless some one among us whom we
must produce for an interpreter.

1 *Soldier.* Good captain, let me be th'interpreter.

2 *Lord.* Art not acquainted with him? knows he not
thy voice?

10 1 *Soldier.* No, sir, I warrant you.

2 *Lord.* But what linsey-woolsey hast thou to speak
to us again?

1 *Soldier.* E'en such as you speak to me.

2 *Lord.* He must think us some band of strangers i'the
adversary's entertainment. Now he hath a smack of
all neighbouring languages; therefore we must every
one be a man of his own fancy; not to know what we
speak one to another, so we seem to know, is to know
straight our purpose: choughs' language, gabble enough,
20 and good enough. As for you, interpreter, you must
seem very politic. But couch, ho! here he comes—to
beguile two hours in a sleep, and then to return and
swear the lies he forges.

PAROLLES comes along the hedge

Parolles. Ten o'clock: within these three hours 'twill
be time enough to go home. What shall I say I have
done? It must be a very plausive invention that carries
it. They begin to smoke me, and disgraces have of late

knocked too often at my door...I find my tongue is too foolhardy, but my heart hath the fear of Mars before it and of his creatures, not daring the reports of my 30 tongue.

(2 Lord. This is the first truth that e'er thine own tongue was guilty of.

Parolles. What the devil should move me to undertake the recovery of this drum, being not ignorant of the impossibility, and knowing I had no such purpose? I must give myself some hurts, and say I got them in exploit...Yet slight ones will not carry it. They will say, 'Came you off with so little?' And great ones I dare not give. Wherefore, what's the instance? Tongue, I must 40 put you into a butter-woman's mouth, and buy myself another of Bajazet's †mate, if you prattle me into these perils.

(2 Lord. Is it possible he should know what he is, and be that he is?

Parolles. I would the cutting of my garments would serve the turn, or the breaking of my Spanish sword.

(2 Lord. We cannot afford you so.

Parolles. Or the baring of my beard, and to say it was in stratagem.

(2 Lord. 'Twould not do.   50

Parolles. Or to drown my clothes, and say I was stripped.

(2 Lord. Hardly serve.

Parolles. Though I swore I leaped from the window of the citadel—

(2 Lord. How deep?

Parolles. Thirty fathom.

(2 Lord. Three great oaths would scarce make that be believed.

Parolles. I would I had any drum of the enemy's, 60 I would swear I recovered it.

(2 *Lord.* You shall hear one anon.

Parolles. A drum now of the enemy's—

　　　[*they strike up the drum and rush upon him*

2 *Lord.* Throca movousus, cargo, cargo, cargo.

All. Cargo, cargo, cargo, villianda par corbo, cargo.

Parolles. O! ransom, ransom! Do not hide mine eyes.

　　　[*they bind him and blindfold his eyes in his scarf*

　1 *Soldier.* Boskos thromuldo boskos.

Parolles. I know you are the Muskos' regiment.

And I shall lose my life for want of language.

70 If there be here German, or Dane, low Dutch,

Italian, or French, let him speak to me,

I will discover that which shall undo

The Florentine.

　1 *Soldier.*　　　　Boskos vauvado—

I understand thee, and can speak thy tongue:

Kerelybonto, sir,

Betake thee to thy faith, for seventeen poniards

Are at thy bosom.

　　Parolles.　　　　O!

　1 *Soldier.*　　　　O, pray, pray, pray!

Manka revania dulche.

　2 *Lord.* Oscorbidulchos volivorco.

80　1 *Soldier.* The general is content to spare thee yet,

And, hoodwinked as thou art, will lead thee on

To gather from thee. Haply thou mayst inform

Something to save thy life.

　　Parolles.　　　　O, let me live!

And all the secrets of our camp I'll show,

Their force, their purposes: nay, I'll speak that

Which you will wonder at.

　1 *Soldier.*　　　　But wilt thou faithfully?

Parolles. If I do not, damn me.

　1 *Soldier.*　　　　Acordo linta.

Come on, thou art granted space.

       [the interpreter and other soldiers carry off
         Parolles, the drum beating

  2 *Lord.* Go, tell the Count Rousillon, and
     my brother,
We have caught the woodcock, and will keep
     him muffled   90
Till we do hear from them.

  2 *Soldier.*   Captain, I will.

  2 *Lord.* A' will betray us all unto ourselves—
Inform 'em that.

  2 *Soldier.*   So I will, sir.

  2 *Lord.* Till then, I'll keep him dark, and
     safely locked.   *[they go*

[4. 2.] *A room in the Widow's house at Florence*

            BERTRAM *and* DIANA

Bertram. They told me that your name was Fontibell.

Diana. No, my good lord, Diana.

Bertram.   'Titled goddess!
And worth it, with addition...But, fair soul,
In your fine frame hath love no quality?
If the quick fire of youth light not your mind,
You are no maiden but a monument.
When you are dead, you should be such a one
As you are now, for you are cold and stern;
And now you should be as your mother was
When your sweet self was got.   10

  Diana. She then was honest.

  Bertram.   So should you be.

  Diana.   No:
My mother did but duty—such, my lord,
As you owe to your wife.

Bertram.   No more o' that:
I prithee, do not strive against my vows:
I was compelled to her, but I love thee
By love's own sweet constraint, and will for ever
Do thee all rights of service.
Diana.   Ay, so you serve us
Till we serve you: but when you have our roses,
You barely leave our thorns to prick ourselves,
20 And mock us with our bareness.
Bertram.   How have I sworn!
Diana. 'Tis not the many oaths that makes the truth,
But the plain single vow that is vowed true:
What is not holy, that we swear not by,
But take the High'st to witness: then, pray you, tell me,
If I should swear by Jove's great attributes
I loved you dearly, would you believe my oaths
When I did love you ill? This has no holding,
To swear by Him whom I protest to love,
That I will work against Him. Therefore your oaths
30 Are words and poor, conditions but unsealed,
At least in my opinion.
Bertram.   Change it, change it;
Be not so holy-cruel: love is holy,
And my integrity ne'er knew the crafts
That you do charge men with...Stand no more off,
But give thyself unto my sick desires,
Who then recover. Say thou art mine, and ever
My love as it begins shall so persever.
Diana. †I see that men make rope's in such a scarre,
That we'll forsake ourselves. Give me that ring.
40 *Bertram.* I'll lend it thee, my dear; but have
          no power
To give it from me.
Diana.   Will you not, my lord?

Bertram. It is an honour 'longing to our house,
Bequeathéd down from many ancestors,
Which were the greatest obloquy i'th' world
In me to lose.
    Diana.   Mine honour's such a ring,
My chastity's the jewel of our house,
Bequeathéd down from many ancestors,
Which were the greatest obloquy i'th' world
In me to lose. Thus your own proper wisdom
Brings in the champion Honour on my part,   50
Against your vain assault.
    Bertram.   Here, take my ring.
My house, mine honour, yea, my life be thine,
And I'll be bid by thee.   *[she takes the ring*
   Diana. When midnight comes, knock at my
        chamber window:
I'll order take my mother shall not hear.
Now will I charge you in the band of truth,
When you have conquered my yet maiden bed,
Remain there but an hour, nor speak to me:
My reasons are most strong, and you shall know them
When back again this ring shall be delivered: 60
And on your finger in the night I'll put
Another ring, that what in time proceeds
May token to the future our past deeds.
Adieu till then, then fail not: you have won
A wife of me, though there my hope be done.
   Bertram. A heaven on earth I have won by
        wooing thee.
   Diana. For which live long to thank both heaven
        and me!   *[he goes*
You may so in the end.
My mother told me just how he would woo,
As if she sat in's heart. She says all men   70

Have the like oaths: he had sworn to marry me
When his wife's dead; therefore I'll lie with him
When I am buried. Since Frenchmen are so braid,
Marry that will, I live and die a maid:
Only in this disguise I think't no sin
To cozen him that would unjustly win.   [*she goes*

[4. 3.]   *A tent in the Florentine camp*

  The two French Lords, and two or three soldiers

2 *Lord.* You have not given him his mother's letter?

1 *Lord.* I have delivered it an hour since. There is
something in't that stings his nature; for on the reading
it he changed almost into another man.

2 *Lord.* He has much worthy blame laid upon him
for shaking off so good a wife and so sweet a lady.

1 *Lord.* Especially he hath incurred the everlasting
displeasure of the king, who had even tuned his bounty
to sing happiness to him. I will tell you a thing, but
10 you shall let it dwell darkly with you.

2 *Lord.* When you have spoken it, 'tis dead, and I am
the grave of it.

1 *Lord.* He hath perverted a young gentlewoman
here in Florence, of a most chaste renown, and this
night he fleshes his will in the spoil of her honour: he
hath given her his monumental ring, and thinks himself
made in the unchaste composition.

2 *Lord.* Now, God †lay our rebellion! as we are ourselves, what things are we!
20 1 *Lord.* Merely our own traitors. And as in the
common course of all treasons, we still see them reveal
themselves, till they attain to their abhorred ends; so he
that in this action contrives against his own nobility
in his proper stream o'erflows himself.

2 *Lord.* Is it not meant damnable in us, to be trumpeters of our unlawful intents? We shall not then have his company to-night?

1 *Lord.* Not till after midnight; for he is dieted to his hour.

2 *Lord.* That approaches apace: I would gladly have 30 him see his company anatomized, that he might take a measure of his own judgement, wherein so curiously he had set this counterfeit.

1 *Lord.* We will not meddle with him till he come; for his presence must be the whip of the other.

2 *Lord.* In the mean time, what hear you of these wars?

1 *Lord.* I hear there is an overture of peace.

2 *Lord.* Nay, I assure you, a peace concluded.

1 *Lord.* What will Count Rousillon do then? will he travel higher, or return again into France?   40

2 *Lord.* I perceive, by this demand, you are not altogether of his council.

1 *Lord.* Let it be forbid, sir, so should I be a great deal of his act.

2 *Lord.* Sir, his wife some two months since fled from his house: her pretence is a pilgrimage to S. Jaques le Grand; which holy undertaking with most austere sanctimony she accomplished: and, there residing, the tenderness of her nature became as a prey to her grief; in fine, made a groan of her last breath, and now she 50 sings in heaven.

1 *Lord.* How is this justified?

2 *Lord.* The stronger part of it by her own letters, which makes her story true, even to the point of her death: her death itself, which could not be her office to say is come, was faithfully confirmed by the rector of the place.

1 *Lord.* Hath the count all this intelligence?

2 *Lord.* Ay, and the particular confirmations, point
60 from point, to the full arming of the verity.

1 *Lord.* I am heartily sorry that he'll be glad of this.

2 *Lord.* How mightily sometimes we make us comforts of our losses!

1 *Lord.* And how mightily some other times we
drown our gain in tears! The great dignity that his
valour hath here acquired for him shall at home be
encountered with a shame as ample.

2 *Lord.* The web of our life is of a mingled yarn, good
and ill together: our virtues would be proud, if our
70 faults whipped them not, and our crimes would
despair, if they were not cherished by our virtues.

A servant comes in

How now! where's your master?

Servant. He met the duke in the street, sir, of whom
he hath taken a solemn leave; his lordship will next
morning for France. The duke hath offered him letters
of commendations to the king.

2 *Lord.* They shall be no more than needful there, if
they were more than they can commend.

1 *Lord.* They cannot be too sweet for the king's
80 tartness.

BERTRAM enters

Here's his lordship now. How now, my lord, is't not
after midnight?

Bertram. I have to-night dispatched sixteen businesses,
a month's length a-piece, by an abstract of success:
I have congied with the duke, done my adieu with his
nearest, buried a wife, mourned for her, writ to my lady
mother I am returning, entertained my convoy, and
between these main parcels of dispatch, effected many
nicer needs: the last was the greatest, but that I have not
90 ended yet.

2 *Lord.* If the business be of any difficulty, and this morning your departure hence, it requires haste of your lordship.

Bertram. I mean, the business is not ended, as fearing to hear of it hereafter...But shall we have this dialogue between the Fool and the Soldier? Come, bring forth this counterfeit module, has deceived me like a double-meaning prophesier.

2 *Lord.* Bring him forth. [*a soldier goes out*] Has sat i'th' stocks all night, poor gallant knave.   100

Bertram. No matter, his heels have deserved it, in usurping his spurs so long. How does he carry himself?

2 *Lord.* I have told your lordship already; the stocks carry him. But to answer you as you would be understood, he weeps like a wench that had shed her milk. He hath confessed himself to Morgan, whom he supposes to be a friar, from the time of his remembrance to this very instant disaster of his setting i'th' stocks: and what think you he hath confessed?

Bertram. Nothing of me, has a'?   110

2 *Lord.* His confession is taken, and it shall be read to his face. If your lordship be in't, as I believe you are, you must have the patience to hear it.

Soldiers bring in PAROLLES, *with his Interpreter*

Bertram. A plague upon him! muffled! he can say nothing of me.

1 *Lord.* Hush! hush! Hoodman comes! Porto-tartarossa.

Interpreter. He calls for the tortures. What will you say without 'em?

Parolles. I will confess what I know without con- 120 straint. If ye pinch me like a pasty, I can say no more.

Interpreter. Bosko chimurcho.

1 *Lord.* Boblibindo chicurmurco.

Interpreter. You are a merciful general...Our general bids you answer to what I shall ask you out of a note.

Parolles. And truly, as I hope to live.

Interpreter. 'First demand of him how many horse the duke is strong.' What say you to that?

Parolles. Five or six thousand, but very weak and 130 unserviceable: the troops are all scattered, and the commanders very poor rogues, upon my reputation and credit, and as I hope to live.

Interpreter. Shall I set down your answer so?

Parolles. Do, I'll take the sacrament on't, how and which way you will. [*the interpreter writes*

(*Bertram.* All's one to him. What a past-saving slave is this!

(1 *Lord.* Y'are deceived, my lord, this is Monsieur Parolles, the gallant militarist—that was his own 140 phrase—that had the whole theoric of war in the knot of his scarf, and the practice in the chape of his dagger.

(2 *Lord.* I will never trust a man again for keeping his sword clean, nor believe he can have every thing in him by wearing his apparel neatly.

Interpreter [*looks up*]. Well, that's set down.

Parolles. Five or six thousand horse, I said—I will say true—or thereabouts, set down, for I'll speak truth.

(1 *Lord.* He's very near the truth in this.

(*Bertram.* But I con him no thanks for't, in the nature 150 he delivers it.

Parolles. Poor rogues, I pray you, say.

Interpreter. Well, that's set down.

Parolles. I humbly thank you, sir—a truth's a truth—the rogues are marvellous poor.

Interpreter. 'Demand of him, of what strength they are a-foot.' What say you to that?

Parolles. By my troth, sir, if I were to †leave this

present hour, I will tell true. Let me see—Spurio a
hundred and fifty, Sebastian so many, Corambus so
many, Jaques so many; Guiltian, Cosmo, Lodowick, 160
and Gratii, two hundred and fifty each: mine own
company, Chitopher, Vaumond, Bentii, two hundred
and fifty each: so that the muster-file, rotten and sound,
upon my life, amounts not to fifteen thousand poll, half
of the which dare not shake the snow from off their
cassocks, lest they shake themselves to pieces.

(*Bertram*. What shall be done to him?

(*1 Lord*. Nothing, but let him have thanks. [*to interpreter*] Demand of him my condition, and what credit
I have with the duke.   170

Interpreter. Well, that's set down.
'You shall demand of him, whether one Captain
Dumain be i'th' camp, a Frenchman: what his reputation is with the duke, what his valour, honesty, and
expertness in wars; or whether he thinks it were not
possible, with well-weighing sums of gold, to corrupt
him to a revolt.'
What say you to this? what do you know of it?

Parolles. I beseech you, let me answer to the particular
of the inter'gatories. Demand them singly.   180

Interpreter. Do you know this Captain Dumain?

Parolles. I know him, a' was a botcher's prentice in
Paris, from whence he was whipped for getting the
shrieve's fool with child—a dumb innocent, that could
not say him nay.   [*Dumain is about to strike him*

(*Bertram*. Nay, by your leave, hold your hands,
though I know his brains are forfeit to the next tile that
falls.

Interpreter. Well, is this captain in the Duke of
Florence's camp?   190

Parolles. Upon my knowledge he is, and lousy.

⟨1 *Lord*. Nay, look not so upon me; we shall hear of your lordship anon.

Interpreter. What is his reputation with the duke?

Parolles. The duke knows him for no other but a poor officer of mine, and writ to me this other day to turn him out o'th' band. I think I have his letter in my pocket.

Interpreter. Marry, we'll search.   [*he does so*

200 *Parolles*. In good sadness, I do not know—either it is there, or it is upon a file with the duke's other letters in my tent.

Interpreter. Here 'tis, here's a paper, shall I read it to you?

Parolles. I do not know if it be it or no.

⟨*Bertram*. Our interpreter does it well.

⟨1 *Lord*. Excellently.

Interpreter [*reads the paper*]. 'Dian, the count's a fool, and full of gold'—

Parolles. That is not the duke's letter, sir; that is an 210 advertisement to a proper maid in Florence, one Diana, to take heed of the allurement of one Count Rousillon, a foolish idle boy: but for all that very ruttish. I pray you, sir, put it up again.

Interpreter. Nay, I'll read it first, by your favour.

Parolles. My meaning in't, I protest, was very honest in the behalf of the maid: for I knew the young count to be a dangerous and lascivious boy, who is a whale to virginity, and devours up all the fry it finds.

⟨*Bertram*. Damnable both-sides rogue!

220 *Interpreter* [*reads*]. 'When he swears oaths, bid him drop gold, and take it;

After he scores, he never pays the score:

Half won is match well made, match and well make it,

He ne'er pays after-debts, take it before.

And say a soldier, Dian, told thee this:
Men are to mell with, boys are but to kiss:
For count of this, the count's a fool, I know it,
Who pays before, but not when he does owe it.

      Thine, as he vowed to thee in thine ear,
                                  PAROLLES.'

 Bertram. He shall be whipped through the army with 230
this rhyme in's forehead.

 2 Lord. This is your devoted friend, sir, the manifold
linguist, and the armipotent soldier.

 Bertram. I could endure any thing before but a cat,
and now he's a cat to me.

 Interpreter. I perceive, sir, by the general's looks, we
shall be fain to hang you.

 Parolles. My life, sir, in any case! not that I am afraid
to die, but that my offences being many I would repent
out the remainder of nature. Let me live, sir, in a 240
dungeon, i'th' stocks, or any where, so I may live.

 Interpreter. We'll see what may be done, so you
confess freely; therefore, once more to this Captain
Dumain: you have answered to his reputation with the
duke and to his valour: what is his honesty?

 Parolles. He will steal, sir, an egg out of a cloister:
for rapes and ravishments he parallels Nessus. He
professes not keeping of oaths, in breaking 'em he
is stronger than Hercules. He will lie, sir, with such
volubility, that you would think truth were a fool: 250
drunkenness is his best virtue, for he will be swine-
drunk, and in his sleep he does little harm, save to his
bed-clothes about him; but they know his conditions
and lay him in straw. I have but little more to say, sir,
of his honesty—he has every thing that an honest man
should not have; what an honest man should have, he
has nothing.

                                             PSAW

(1 *Lord.* I begin to love him for this.

(*Bertram.* For this description of thine honesty? A
260 pox upon him for me, he's more and more a cat.

Interpreter. What say you to his expertness in war?

Parolles. Faith, sir, has led the drum before the
English tragedians; to belie him, I will not, and more
of his soldiership I know not, except in that country
he had the honour to be the officer at a place there called
Mile-end, to instruct for the doubling of files. I would
do the man what honour I can, but of this I am not
certain.

(1 *Lord.* He hath out-villained villainy so far, that
270 the rarity redeems him.

(*Bertram.* A pox on him, he's a cat still.

Interpreter. His qualities being at this poor price, I
need not to ask you, if gold will corrupt him to revolt.

Parolles. Sir, for a cardecue he will sell the fee-simple
of his salvation, the inheritance of it; and cut th'entail
from all remainders, and a perpetual succession for it
perpetually.

Interpreter. What's his brother, the other Captain
Dumain?
280 (2 *Lord.* Why does he ask him of me?

Interpreter. What's he?

Parolles. E'en a crow o'th' same nest; not altogether
so great as the first in goodness, but greater a great deal
in evil. He excels his brother for a coward, yet his
brother is reputed one of the best that is. In a retreat
he outruns any lackey; marry, in coming on he has the
cramp.

Interpreter. If your life be saved, will you undertake
to betray the Florentine?
290 *Parolles.* Ay, and the captain of his horse, Count
Rousillon.

Interpreter. I'll whisper with the general, and know his pleasure.

(*Parolles.* I'll no more drumming, a plague of all drums. Only to seem to deserve well, and to beguile the supposition of that lascivious young boy, the count, have I run into this danger: yet, who would have suspected an ambush where I was taken?

Interpreter. There is no remedy, sir, but you must die: the general says, you that have so traitorously discovered 300 the secrets of your army and made such pestiferous reports of men very nobly held, can serve the world for no honest use; therefore you must die. Come, headsman, off with his head.

Parolles. O Lord, sir, let me live, or let me see my death!

Interpreter. That shall you, and take your leave of all your friends...   [*he plucks the scarf from his eyes* So, look about you. Know you any here?

Bertram. Good morrow, noble captain.   310

2 *Lord.* God bless you, Captain Parolles.

1 *Lord.* God save you, noble captain.

2 *Lord.* Captain, what greeting will you to my Lord Lafeu? I am for France.

1 *Lord.* Good captain, will you give me a copy of the sonnet you writ to Diana in behalf of the Count Rousillon? an I were not a very coward, I'd compel it of you, but fare you well.

       [*Bertram and the Lords leave the tent*
Interpreter. You are undone, captain, all but your scarf—that has a knot on't yet.   320

Parolles. Who cannot be crushed with a plot?

Interpreter. If you could find out a country where but women were that had received so much shame, you might begin an impudent nation. Fare ye well,

sir, I am for France too, we shall speak of you
there.   *[he goes*

   Parolles. Yet am I thankful: if my heart were great,
'Twould burst at this...Captain I'll be no more,
But I will eat and drink, and sleep as soft
330 As captain shall: simply the thing I am
Shall make me live. Who knows himself a braggart,
Let him fear this; for it will come to pass
That every braggart shall be found an ass.
Rust, sword! cool, blushes! and, Parolles, live
Safest in shame! being fooled, by foolery thrive!
There's place and means for every man alive.
I'll after them.   *[he goes*

[4. 4.] *The room in the Widow's house at Florence*

HELENA, WIDOW, *and* DIANA

   Helena. That you may well perceive I have not
          wronged you,
One of the greatest in the Christian world
Shall be my surety: 'fore whose throne 'tis needful,
Ere I can perfect mine intents, to kneel.
Time was, I did him a desiréd office,
Dear almost as his life, which gratitude
Through flinty Tartar's bosom would peep forth,
And answer, thanks. I duly am informed
His grace is at Marseillës, to which place
10 We have convenient convoy...You must know,
I am supposéd dead: the army breaking,
My husband hies him home, where, heaven aiding,
And by the leave of my good lord the king,
We'll be before our welcome.
   Widow.   Gentle madam,
You never had a servant to whose trust

Your business was more welcome.

Helena.   Nor you, mistress,
Ever a friend whose thoughts more truly labour
To recompense your love: doubt not but heaven
Hath brought me up to be your daughter's dower,
As it hath fated her to be my motive   20
And helper to a husband. But, O strange men,
That can such sweet use make of what they hate,
When saucy trusting of the cozened thoughts
Defiles the pitchy night! so lust doth play
With what it loathes, for that which is away.
But more of this hereafter...You, Diana,
Under my poor instructions yet must suffer
Something in my behalf.

Diana.   Let death and honesty
Go with your impositions, I am yours
Upon your will to suffer.

Helena.   Yet, I pray you...   30
†But with the word, that time will bring on summer,
When briars shall have leaves as well as thorns,
And be as sweet as sharp...We must away,
Our waggon is prepared, and time revives us.
'All's well that ends well,' still the fine's the crown;
Whate'er the course, the end is the renown.   [*they go*

[4. 5.]   *A room in the palace of Rousillon*

COUNTESS, LAFEU, *and* CLOWN

Lafeu. No, no, no, your son was misled with a snipt-
taffeta fellow there, whose villanous saffron would have
made all the unbaked and doughy youth of a nation in
his colour: your daughter-in-law had been alive at this
hour, and your son here at home, more advanced by
the king than by that red-tailed humble-bee I speak of.

Countess. I would I had not known him—it was the death of the most virtuous gentlewoman that ever nature had praise for creating. If she had partaken of
10 my flesh, and cost me the dearest groans of a mother, I could not have owed her a more rooted love.

Lafeu. 'Twas a good lady, 'twas a good lady. We may pick a thousand salads ere we light on such another herb.

Clown. Indeed, sir, she was the sweet-marjoram of the salad, or rather, the herb of grace.

Lafeu. They are †knot-herbs, you knave, they are nose-herbs.

Clown. I am no great Nebuchadnezzar, sir, I have
20 not much skill in grass.

Lafeu. Whether dost thou profess thyself, a knave or a fool?

Clown. A fool, sir, at a woman's service, and a knave at a man's.

Lafeu. Your distinction?

Clown. I would cozen the man of his wife, and do his service.

Lafeu. So you were a knave at his service, indeed.

Clown. And I would give his wife my bauble, sir,
30 to do her service.

Lafeu. I will subscribe for thee, thou art both knave and fool.

Clown. At your service.

Lafeu. No, no, no.

Clown. Why, sir, if I cannot serve you, I can serve as great a prince as you are.

Lafeu. Who's that? a Frenchman?

Clown. Faith, sir, a' has an English name, but his fisnamy is more hotter in France than there.

40 *Lafeu.* What prince is that?

Clown. The Black Prince, sir, alias the prince of dark-
ness, alias the devil.

Lafeu. Hold thee, there's my purse. I give thee not
this to suggest thee from thy master thou talk'st of—
serve him still.

Clown. I am a woodland fellow, sir, that always loved
a great fire, and the master I speak of ever keeps a good
fire. But, sure, he is the prince of the world, let his
nobility remain in's court. I am for the house with the
narrow gate, which I take to be too little for pomp to 50
enter: some that humble themselves may, but the many
will be too chill and tender, and they'll be for the
flowery way that leads to the broad gate and the great
fire.

Lafeu. Go thy ways, I begin to be aweary of thee,
and I tell thee so before, because I would not fall out
with thee. Go thy ways, let my horses be well looked
to, without any tricks.

Clown. If I put any tricks upon 'em, sir, they shall
be jades' tricks, which are their own right by the law 60
of nature.   [*he goes*

Lafeu. A shrewd knave and an unhappy.

Countess. So a' is. My lord that's gone made himself
much sport out of him: by his authority he remains
here, which he thinks is a patent for his sauciness, and
indeed he has no pace, but runs where he will.

Lafeu. I like him well, 'tis not amiss...And I was
about to tell you, since I heard of the good lady's death
and that my lord your son was upon his return home,
I moved the king my master to speak in the behalf of 70
my daughter—which, in the minority of them both, his
majesty out of a self-gracious remembrance did first
propose. His highness hath promised me to do it—and,
to stop up the displeasure he hath conceived against

your son, there is no fitter matter. How does your ladyship like it?

Countess. With very much content, my lord, and I
wish it happily effected.

Lafeu. His highness comes post from Marscilles, of
80 as able body as when he numbered thirty—a' will be
here to-morrow, or I am deceived by him that in such
intelligence hath seldom failed.

Countess. It rejoices me, that I hope I shall see him
ere I die. I have letters that my son will be here to-
night: I shall beseech your lordship to remain with me
till they meet together.

Lafeu. Madam, I was thinking with what manners
I might safely be admitted.

Countess. You need but plead your honourable
90 privilege.

Lafeu. Lady, of that I have made a bold charter, but
I thank my God it holds yet.

CLOWN *returns*

Clown. O madam, yonder's my lord your son with
a patch of velvet on's face—whether there be a scar
under't or no, the velvet knows, but 'tis a goodly patch
of velvet—his left cheek is a cheek of two pile and a half,
but his right cheek is worn bare.

Lafeu. A scar nobly got, or a noble scar, is a good
livery of honour—so belike is that.

100 *Clown.* But it is your carbonadoed face.

Lafeu. Let us go see your son, I pray you. I long to
talk with the young noble soldier.

Clown. Faith, there's a dozen of 'em, with delicate
fine hats and most courteous feathers, which bow the
head, and nod at every man.   [*they go*

[5. 1.]   *A street in Marseilles*

'*HELENA, WIDOW, and DIANA, with two attendants*'

Helena. But this exceeding posting day and night
Must wear your spirits low—we cannot help it:
But since you have made the days and nights as one,
To wear your gentle limbs in my affairs,
Be bold you do so grow in my requital
As nothing can unroot you.

'*Enter a gentle astringer*'

In happy time—
This man may help me to his majesty's ear,
If he would spend his power. God save you, sir.
  Gentleman. And you.
  Helena. Sir, I have seen you in the court of France.   10
  Gentleman. I have been sometimes there.
  Helena. I do presume, sir, that you are not fall'n
From the report that goes upon your goodness,
And therefore, goaded with most sharp occasions,
Which lay nice manners by, I put you to
The use of your own virtues, for the which
I shall continue thankful.
  Gentleman.   What's your will?
  Helena. That it will please you
To give this poor petition to the king,
And aid me with that store of power you have   20
To come into his presence.   [*she gives him a paper*
  Gentleman. The king's not here.
  Helena.   Not here, sir!
  Gentleman.   Not indeed,
He hence removed last night, and with more haste
Than is his use.

Widow. Lord, how we lose our pains!

Helena. 'All's well that ends well' yet,
Though time seem so adverse and means unfit....
I do beseech you, whither is he gone?

Gentleman. Marry, as I take it, to Rousillon,
Whither I am going.

Helena.   I do beseech you, sir,
30 Since you are like to see the king before me,
Commend the paper to his gracious hand,
Which I presume shall render you no blame
But rather make you thank your pains for it.
I will come after you with what good speed
Our means will make us means.

Gentleman.   This I'll do for you.

Helena. And you shall find yourself to be
      well thanked,
Whate'er falls more. We must to horse again.
Go, go, provide.   [*they hurry away*

[5.2.] *In the park near the palace of Rousillon*

CLOWN and PAROLLES

Parolles. Good Master Lavache, give my Lord Lafeu
this letter. I have ere now, sir, been better known to
you, when I have held familiarity with fresher clothes;
but I am now, sir, muddied in fortune's mood, and
smell somewhat strong of her strong displeasure.

Clown. Truly, fortune's displeasure is but sluttish, if
it smell so strongly as thou speak'st of: I will henceforth
eat no fish of fortune's butt'ring. Prithee, allow the
wind.

10 *Parolles.* Nay, you need not to stop your nose, sir;
I spake but by a metaphor.

Clown. Indeed, sir, if your metaphor stink, I will

stop my nose, or against any man's metaphor. Prithee, get thee further.

Parolles. Pray you, sir, deliver me this paper.

Clown. Foh! prithee, stand away: a paper from fortune's close-stool to give to a nobleman! Look, here he comes himself.

LAFEU *approaches*

Here is a pur of fortune's, sir, or of fortune's cat— but not a musk-cat—that has fallen into the unclean 20 fishpond of her displeasure, and, as he says, is muddied withal: pray you, sir, use the carp as you may, for he looks like a poor, decayed, †ingenerous, foolish, rascally knave. I do pity his distress in my similes of comfort, and leave him to your lordship.   [*he goes off*

Parolles. My lord, I am a man whom fortune hath cruelly scratched.

Lafeu. And what would you have me to do? 'tis too late to pare her nails now. Wherein have you played the knave with fortune, that she should scratch you, who 30 of herself is a good lady and would not have knaves thrive long under her? There's a cardecue for you [*he gives him a coin*]: let the justices make you and fortune friends; I am for other business.   [*he passes on*

Parolles. I beseech your honour to hear me one single word.

Lafeu [*turns*]. You beg a single penny more: come, you shall ha't—save your word.
                    [*he gives him another coin*

Parolles. My name, my good lord, is Parolles.

Lafeu. You beg more than one word then. Cox my 40 passion! give me your hand...How does your drum?

Parolles. O my good lord, you were the first that found me.

Lafeu. Was I, in sooth? and I was the first that lost thee.

Parolles. It lies in you, my lord, to bring me in some grace, for you did bring me out. ·

Lafeu. Out upon thee, knave! dost thou put upon me at once both the office of God and the devil? one
50 brings thee in grace and the other brings thee out. [*trumpets sound*] The king's coming, I know by his trumpets. Sirrah, inquire further after me. I had talk of you last night—though you are a fool and a knave, you shall eat. Go to, follow.   [*he hurries away*

Parolles. I praise God for you.   [*he follows*

[5. 3.]   *A room in the palace of Rousillon*

Flourish. Enter KING, COUNTESS, LAFEU, lords, gentlemen, guards, &c.

King. We lost a jewel of her, and our esteem
Was made much poorer by it: but your son,
As mad in folly, lacked the sense to know
Her estimation home.
Countess.   'Tis past, my liege,
And I beseech your majesty to make it
Natural rebellion, done i'th' blaze of youth,
When oil and fire, too strong for reason's force,
O'erbears it and burns on.
King.   My honoured lady,
I have forgiven and forgotten all,
10 Though my revenges were high bent upon him,
And watched the time to shoot.
Lafeu.   This I must say—
But first I beg my pardon—the young lord
Did to his majesty, his mother and his lady
Offence of mighty note; but to himself

The greatest wrong of all. He lost a wife
Whose beauty did astonish the survey
Of richest eyes, whose words all ears took captive,
Whose dear perfection hearts that scorned to serve
Humbly called mistress.

King.   Praising what is lost
Makes the remembrance dear. Well, call him hither— 20
We are reconciled, and the first view shall kill
All repetition: let him not ask our pardon,
The nature of his great offence is dead,
And deeper than oblivion we do bury
Th'incensing relics of it. Let him approach,
A stranger, no offender; and inform him
So 'tis our will he should.

Gentleman.   I shall, my liege. [*he goes out*

King. What says he to your daughter? have
     you spoke?

Lafeu. All that he is hath reference to your highness.

King. Then shall we have a match. I have letters
     sent me,   30
That sets him high in fame.

BERTRAM enters and stands by the door, awaiting
his summons

Lafeu.   He looks well on't.

King. I am not a day of season,
For thou mayst see a sunshine and a hail
In me at once: but to the brightest beams
Distracted clouds give way—so stand thou forth,
The time is fair again.

Bertram [*kneels before him*]. My high-repented
     blames,
Dear sovereign pardon to me.

King.   All is whole,

Not one word more of the consuméd time.
Let's take the instant by the forward top:
40 For we are old, and on our quick'st decrees
Th'inaudible and noiseless foot of Time
Steals ere we can effect them. You remember
The daughter of this lord?
  Bertram. Admiringly, my liege. At first
I stuck my choice upon her, ere my heart
Durst make too bold a herald of my tongue:
Where the impression of mine eye infixing,
Contempt his scornful perspective did lend me,
Which warped the line of every other favour,
50 Scorned a fair colour or expressed it stol'n,
Extended or contracted all proportions
To a most hideous object. Thence it came
That she whom all men praised and whom myself,
Since I have lost, have loved, was in mine eye
The dust that did offend it.
  King.   Well excused:
That thou didst love her, strikes some scores away
From the great compt: but love that comes too late,
Like a remorseful pardon slowly carried,
To the great sender turns a sour offence,
60 Crying 'That's good that's gone'...Our rash faults
Make trivial price of serious things we have,
Not knowing them, until we know their grave.
Oft our displeasures, to ourselves unjust,
Destroy our friends and after weep their dust:
Our own love waking cries to see what's done,
While shameful hate sleeps out the afternoon.
Be this sweet Helen's knell, and now forget her.
Send forth your amorous token for fair Maudlin
The main consents are had, and here we'll stay
70 To see our widower's second marriage-day.

Countess. Which better than the first, O dear
    heaven, bless!
Or, ere they meet, in me, O nature, cesse!
  Lafeu. Come on, my son, in whom my house's name
Must be digested, give a favour from you,
To sparkle in the spirits of my daughter,
That she may quickly come....[*Bertram gives a ring*]
    By my old beard,
And every hair that's on't, Helen that's dead
Was a sweet creature: such a ring as this,
The last that e'er I took her leave at court,
I saw upon her finger.
  Bertram.   Hers it was not.   80
  King. Now pray you, let me see it; for mine eye,
While I was speaking, oft was fastened to't...
    [*he takes it from Lafeu and sets it upon his finger*
This ring was mine, and when I gave it Helen
I bade her, if her fortunes ever stood
Necessitied to help, that by this token
I would relieve her. Had you that craft, to reave her
Of what should stead her most?
  Bertram.   My gracious sovereign,
Howe'er it pleases you to take it so,
The ring was never hers.
  Countess.   Son, on my life,
I have seen her wear it, and she reckoned it   90
At her life's rate.
  Lafeu.   I am sure I saw her wear it.
  Bertram. You are deceived, my lord, she never
    saw it:
In Florence was it from a casement thrown me,
Wrapped in a paper, which contained the name
Of her that threw it: noble she was, and thought
I stood ungaged: but when I had subscribed

To mine own fortune and informed her fully
I could not answer in that course of honour
As she had made the overture, she ceased
100 In heavy satisfaction and would never
Receive the ring again.
  King.   Plutus himself,
That knows the tinct and multiplying med'cine,
Hath not in nature's mystery more science
Than I have in this ring. 'Twas mine, 'twas Helen's,
Whoever gave it you: then, if you know
That you are well acquainted with yourself,
Confess 'twas hers, and by what rough enforcement
You got it from her. She called the saints to surety,
That she would never put it from her finger,
110 Unless she gave it to yourself in bed—
Where you have never come—or sent it us
Upon her great disaster.
  Bertram.   She never saw it.
  King. Thou speak'st it falsely, as I love
    mine honour;
And mak'st conjectural fears to come into me,
Which I would fain shut out. If it should prove
That thou art so inhuman—'twill not prove so...
And yet I know not—thou didst hate her deadly,
And she is dead, which nothing but to close
Her eyes myself could win me to believe,
120 More than to see this ring. Take him away.
          [guards seize Bertram
My fore-past proofs, howe'er the matter fall,
Shall tax my fears of little vanity,
Having vainly feared too little. Away with him,
We'll sift this matter further.
  Bertram.   If you shall prove
This ring was ever hers, you shall as easy

Prove that I husbanded her bed in Florence,
Where yet she never was.   [*the guards lead him away*
 King. I am wrapped in dismal thinkings.

A gentleman enters and presents a paper

 Gentleman.   Gracious sovereign,
Whether I have been to blame or no, I know not,
Here's a petition from a Florentine,   130
Who hath for four or five removes come short
To tender it herself. I undertook it,
Vanquished thereto by the fair grace and speech
Of the poor suppliant, who by this I know
Is here attending: her business looks in her
With an importing visage, and she told me,
In a sweet verbal brief, it did concern
Your highness with herself.
 King [*reads*]. 'Upon his many protestations to marry
me when his wife was dead, I blush to say it, he won 140
me. Now is the Count Rousillon a widower, his vows
are forfeited to me, and my honour's paid to him. He
stole from Florence, taking no leave, and I follow him
to his country for justice: grant it me, O king! in you
it best lies, otherwise a seducer flourishes and a poor
maid is undone.   DIANA CAPULET.'
 Lafeu. I will buy me a son-in-law in a fair, and toll
for this. I'll none of him.
 King. The heavens have thought well on thee, Lafeu,
To bring forth this discov'ry. Seek these suitors...   150
                            [*the gentleman goes*
Go, speedily and bring again the count.
                            [*attendants hurry forth*
I am afeard the life of Helen, lady,
Was foully snatched.
 Countess.   Now, justice on the doers!

The guards return with BERTRAM

King. I wonder, sir, sith wives are monsters to you,
And that you fly them as you swear them lordship,
Yet you desire to marry.

The gentleman returns with WIDOW *and* DIANA

                             What woman's that?
Diana. I am, my lord, a wretched Florentine,
Derivéd from the ancient Capulet.
My suit, as I do understand, you know,
160 And therefore know how far I may be pitied.
    Widow. I am her mother, sir, whose age and honour
Both suffer under this complaint we bring,
And both shall cease, without your remedy.
    King. Come hither, count—do you know
        these women?
    Bertram. My lord, I neither can nor will deny
But that I know them. Do they charge me further?
    Diana. Why do you look so strange upon your wife?
    Bertram. She's none of mine, my lord.
    Diana.   If you shall marry,
You give away this hand, and that is mine;
170 You give away heaven's vows, and those are mine;
You give away myself, which is known mine;
For I by vow am so embodied yours,
That she which marries you must marry me,
Either both or none.
    Lafeu. Your reputation comes too short for my
daughter, you are no husband for her.
    Bertram. My lord, this is a fond and desp'rate
        creature,
Whom sometime I have laughed with: let your highness
Lay a more noble thought upon mine honour,

Than for to think that I would sink it here.   180
  King. Sir, for my thoughts, you have them ill
       to friend
Till your deeds gain them: fairer prove your honour
Than in my thought it lies.
  Diana.   Good my lord,
Ask him upon his oath, if he does think
He had not my virginity.
  King. What say'st thou to her?
  Bertram.   She's impudent, my lord,
And was a common gamester to the camp.
  Diana. He does me wrong, my lord; if I were so,
He might have bought me at a common price.
Do not believe him. O, behold this ring,   190
Whose high respect and rich validity
Did lack a parallel; yet for all that
He gave it to a commoner o'th' camp,
If I be one.
  Countess.   He blushes, and 'tis it!
Of six preceding ancestors, that gem,
Conferred by testament to th' sequent issue,
Hath it been owed and worn. This is his wife,
That ring's a thousand proofs.
  King.   Methought you said
You saw one here in court could witness it.
  Diana. I did, my lord, but loath am to produce   200
So bad an instrument. His name's Parolles.
  Lafeu. I saw the man to-day, if man he be.
  King. Find him, and bring him hither.
                   [Lafeu goes out
  Bertram.   What of him?
He's quoted for a most perfidious slave,
With all the spots o'th' world taxed and deboshed;
Whose nature sickens but to speak a truth.

Am I or that or this for what he'll utter,
That will speak any thing?
 King.   She hath that ring of yours
 Bertram. I think she has: certain it is I liked her,
210 And boarded her i'th' wanton way of youth:
She knew her distance, and did angle for me,
Madding my eagerness with her restraint—
As all impediments in fancy's course
Are motives of more fancy—and in fine
Her infinite cunning with her modern grace
Subdued me to her rate. She got the ring,
And I had that which any inferior might
At market-price have bought.
 Diana.   I must be patient:
You that turned off a first so noble wife,
220 May justly diet me. I pray you yet—
Since you lack virtue I will lose a husband—
Send for your ring, I will return it home,
And give me mine again.
 Bertram.   I have it not.
 King. What ring was yours, I pray you?
 Diana.   Sir, much like
The same upon your finger.
 King. Know you this ring? this ring was his of late.
 Diana. And this was it I gave him, being abed.
 King. The story then goes false, you threw it him
Out of a casement?
 Diana.   I have spoke the truth.

Lafeu returns with Parolles

230 *Bertram*. My lord, I do confess, the ring was hers.
 King. You boggle shrewdly, every feather
  starts you...
Is this the man you speak of?

Diana. Ay, my lord.

King. Tell me, sirrah, but tell me true, I charge you,
Not fearing the displeasure of your master—
Which on your just proceeding I'll keep off—
By him and by this woman here what know you?

Parolles. So please your majesty, my master hath
been an honourable gentleman: tricks he hath had in
him, which gentlemen have.

King. Come, come, to th' purpose: did he love this 240
woman?

Parolles. Faith, sir, he did love her, but how?

King. How, I pray you?

Parolles. He did love her, sir, as a gentleman loves
a woman.

King. How is that?

Parolles. He loved her, sir, and loved her not.

King. As thou art a knave, and no knave. What an
equivocal companion is this!

Parolles. I am a poor man, and at your majesty's 250
command.

Lafeu. He's a good drum, my lord, but a naughty
orator.

Diana. Do you know he promised me marriage?

Parolles. Faith, I know more than I'll speak.

King. But wilt thou not speak all thou know'st?

Parolles. Yes, so please your majesty...I did go
between them as I said—but more than that, he loved
her, for indeed he was mad for her, and talked of Satan,
and of Limbo, and of Furies, and I know not what: 260
yet I was in that credit with them at that time, that I
knew of their going to bed, and of other motions, as
promising her marriage, and things which would derive
me ill will to speak of—therefore I will not speak what
I know.

King. Thou hast spoken all already, unless thou
canst say they are married. But thou art too fine in thy
evidence, therefore stand aside....
This ring, you say, was yours?

Diana.   Ay, my good lord.

270 *King.* Where did you buy it? or who gave it you?

Diana. It was not given me, nor I did not buy it.

King. Who lent it you?

Diana.   It was not lent me neither.

King. Where did you find it then?

Diana.   I found it not.

King. If it were yours by none of all these ways,
How could you give it him?

Diana.   I never gave it him.

Lafeu. This woman's an easy glove, my lord, she
goes off and on at pleasure.

King. This ring was mine, I gave it his first wife.

Diana. It might be yours or hers, for aught I know.

280 *King.* Take her away, I do not like her now,
To prison with her: and away with him.
Unless thou tell'st me where thou hadst this ring,
Thou diest within this hour.

Diana.   I'll never tell you.

King. Take her away.

Diana.   I'll put in bail, my liege.

King. I think thee now some common customer.

Diana [to Lafeu]. By Jove, if ever I knew man,
        'twas you.

King. Wherefore hast thou accused him all this while?

Diana. Because he's guilty, and he is not guilty:
He knows I am no maid, and he'll swear to't:

290 I'll swear I am a maid, and he knows not.
Great king, I am no strumpet, by my life,
I am either maid, or else this old man's wife.

King. She does abuse our ears—to prison with her!
Diana. Good mother, fetch my bail....[*Widow goes*]
      Stay, royal sir,
The jeweller that owes the ring is sent for,
And he shall surety me. But for this lord,
Who hath abused me, as he knows himself,
Though yet he never harmed me, here I quit him.
He knows himself my bed he hath defiled,
And at that time he got his wife with child: 300
Dead though she be, she feels her young one kick:
So there's my riddle—One that's dead is quick.
And now behold the meaning.

          WIDOW returns with HELENA

   King.   Is there no exorcist
Beguiles the truer office of mine eyes?
Is't real that I see?
   Helena.   No, my good lord,
'Tis but the shadow of a wife you see,
The name and not the thing.
   Bertram [*kneels*].   Both, both. O, pardon!
   Helena. O, my good lord, when I was like this maid,
I found you wondrous kind. There is your ring,
And, look you, here's your letter: this it says,   310
'When from my finger you can get this ring,
And are by me with child,' &c. This is done.
Will you be mine, now you are doubly won?
   Bertram. If she, my liege, can make me know
      this clearly,
I'll love her dearly, ever, ever dearly.
   Helena. If it appear not plain and prove untrue,
Deadly divorce step between me and you!
O, my dear mother, do I see you living?
   Lafeu. Mine eyes smell onions, I shall weep anon:

320 [*to Parolles*] Good Tom Drum, lend me a handkercher:
so, I thank thee. Wait on me home, I'll make sport with
thee: let thy curtsies alone, they are scurvy ones.

   King. Let us from point to point this story know,
To make the even truth in pleasure flow...
[*to Diana*] If thou be'st yet a fresh uncroppéd flower,
Choose thou thy husband, and I'll pay thy dower,
For I can guess that by thy honest aid
Thou kept'st a wife herself, thyself a maid.
Of that and all the progress, more and less,
330 Resolvedly more leisure shall express:
All yet seems well, and if it end so meet,
The bitter past, more welcome is the sweet.

   A flourish. The King advances to speak the Epilogue

Epilogue

The king's a beggar now the play is done.
All is well ended, if this suit be won,
That you express content; which we will pay,
With strife to please you, day exceeding day:
Ours be your patience then, and yours our parts,
Your gentle hands lend us, and take our hearts.

                                  [*they go*

GLOSSARY

Note. Where a pun or quibble is intended, the meanings
are distinguished as (*a*) and (*b*)

ABLE FOR (be), be a match for; 1. 1.
66

ACCORDINGLY, in proportion; 2. 5. 9

ACROSS. An expression from the
tilt-yard, implying that the jest
or sally has missed its mark, as
the unskilful tilter breaks his
lance across his opponent's body
instead of goring him with its
point (cf. *A.Y.L.* note 3. 4. 39–
41); 2. 1. 67

ACT, activity, the life of action;
1. 2. 30

ADDITION, title, style of address;
2. 3. 130

ADMIRATION, wonder, marvel; 2. 1.
88

ADOPTIOUS, assumed, adopted (a
coinage of Shakespeare's); 1. 1.
174

ADVERTISEMENT, warning, admoni-
tion; 4. 3. 210

ADVICE, prudence, forethought;
3. 4. 19

AMES-ACE, i.e. ambs-ace, double
ace, the lowest possible throw
at dice; 2. 3. 82

AMPLE, adv. completely (cf. *Tim.*
1. 2. 136 'how ample you're
beloved'); 3. 5. 42

ANATOMIZE, lit. dissect (surg.),
lay open minutely, expose; 4. 3.
31

APPEACH, turn informer, peach.
'Peach' and 'appeach' are originally the same word, but 'appeach'
generally means (both in Sh. and

elsewhere) to accuse or charge
with a crime, without any im-
plication of treachery on the
part of the accuser; 1. 3. 188

APPLICATION, medical treatment;
1. 2. 74

APPOINTMENTS, engagements, business. Bertram may be referring
to his equipment for the journey,
'appointment' being a common
word for equipage; 2. 5. 69

APPREHENSIVE, quick to apprehend
or receive impressions; 1. 2. 60

APPROOF, confirmed reputation,
general recognition (cf. *approve*);
1. 2. 50; 2. 5. 3

APPROVE, test, confirm, prove; 1. 2.
10; 1. 3. 225; 3. 7. 13

ARAISE, raise from the dead. An
archaic word chosen to suit
'King Pepin' (O.E.D. quotes no
later example); 2. 1. 76

ARGUMENT, subject-matter of conversation; 2. 3. 7

ARMIPOTENT, mighty in arms (a
conventional epithet, here ludicrous, usually applied to Mars;
cf. Chaucer, *Kt's Tale,* 1982
and *L.L.L.* G.); 4. 3. 233

ARTIST, man of skill or learning,
(here) physician; 2. 3. 10

ASTRINGER, i.e. austringer, falconer,
keeper of goshawks; poss. misp.
of 'Usher' (cf. Chambers, *Wm.
Sh.* 1, 450); 5. 1. 6 S.D.

AUTHENTIC, legally qualified or
authorised; 2. 3. 14

BAND, bond, promise (cf. *R. II*, 1. 1. 2 'thy oath and band'); 4. 2. 56

BARE, shave; 4. 1. 48

BARNES, bairns, children (? with a quibble upon 'barns'); 1. 3. 25

BATE, remit, except; 2. 1. 13; 2. 3. 226

BAUBLE, i.e. the fool's stick, ending in a fool's head. Here used in an equivocal sense (cf. *R. & J.* 2. 4. 97); 4. 5. 29

BEFORE ME, (*a*) in my presence, (*b*) upon my soul; 2. 4. 30

BESTOW, confer as a gift. Most edd. interpret 'put away'; 1. 3. 222

BLOOD, i.e. passion (cf. *M.V.* 1. 2. 17); 1. 3. 128

BOARD, accost, make advances to (the orig. nautical meaning still felt in the word, conveying the sense of hostile attack); 5. 3. 210

BOGGLE, shy like a startled horse, take alarm; 5. 3. 231

BOLD (be), be assured (cf. *L.L.L.* 2. 1. 18 'Bold of your worthiness'); 5. 1. 5

BOTCHER, a tailor who does repairs; 4. 3. 182

BRAID. 'Of doubtful meaning and origin' (O.E.D.). Possibly Sc. for 'broad' = loose, lascivious; 4. 2. 73

BRAVELY, i.e. (i) with a light heart; 2. 1. 29; 2. 3. 303; (ii) at a high rate or value; 3. 5. 51

BRAVING, defiant; 1. 2. 3

BREAK, break up, disband; 4. 4. 11

BREATH, speech, utterance (cf. *Ado*, 5. 1. 256; *Meas.* 5. 1. 121); 2. 1. 148

BREATHE (one's self), take exercise; 2. 3. 259

BREATHING, exercise; 1. 2. 17

BRIEF, (i) legal document, contract; 2. 3. 182; (ii) a summary; 5. 3. 137

BROKE, to trade as a procurer. 'A broker in our author's time meant a bawd or pimp' Malone (cf. *Ham.* 1. 3. 127–30 'brokers ...like sanctified and pious bawds'); 3. 5. 70

BROKEN, i.e. gap-toothed; 2. 3. 63

BY, about, concerning; 5. 3. 236

CALENDAR, register; 1. 3. 5

CANARY, a lively Spanish dance; 2. 1. 74

CAPABLE, ready to learn (cf. Hooker, *Eccl. Pol.* v. lvii. 1 'infants which are not capable of instruction,' and *L.L.L.* 4. 2. 82); 1. 1. 97, 209

CAPRICCIO, It., caprice (the word 'caprice' did not enter the language before 1660); 2. 3. 297

CAPTIOUS, (*a*) fallacious, deceptive, (*b*) receptive; 1. 3. 199

CARBONADOED, slashed or scored (like a piece of meat for broiling); 4. 5. 100

CARDECUE, Fr. 'quart d'écu' (a silver coin = c. 1*s*. 6*d*.); 4. 3. 274; 5. 2. 32

CARP, (*a*) freshwater fish commonly bred in ponds, (*b*) talkative person (v. 'carp' vb. O.E.D.); 5. 2. 22

CASE, vb. skin, strip (a term in venery. Cf. Turbervile, *Booke of Hunting*, 1576, p. 241 'The Harte and all manner of Deare are flayne....The Hare is stryped and...the Bore also: the Foxe, Badgerd and all other vermine are cased'); 3. 6. 98

CASE, sb. cause, suit (? with a quibble upon 'case' = body; cf. *Tw. Nt.* 5. 1. 168); 1. 3. 23

CASSOCK, long loose cloak, cloak worn by musketeers and other soldiers in 16th–17th cent. (the ecclesiastical sense is app. unknown before 1660); 4. 3. 166

CATASTROPHE, lit. the dénouement of a play, conclusion of any kind, tail-end; 1. 2. 57

CAUSE, disease, sickness (v. O.E.D. 'cause' 12, and cf. *Cor.* 3. 1. 235 'Leave us to cure this cause'); 2. 1. 111

CESSE, an archaic form of 'cease' (cf. *Ham.* 3. 3. 15 (Q2) 'The cesse of majesty'); 5. 3. 72

CHALLENGE, lay claim to, demand as a right; 2. 3. 137

CHAPE, 'the metal plate or mounting of a scabbard or sheath; particularly that which covers the point' (O.E.D.); 4. 3. 141

CHECK, reproach, rebuke; 1. 1. 68

CHOICE, 'special value, estimation' (O.E.D., quoting this as its only instance of the meaning). Probably a coinage from 'choice' adj. which is frequent in Sh.; 3. 7. 26

CHOUGH, 'a bird of the crow family; formerly applied somewhat widely to all the smaller chattering species, but especially to the common jackdaw' (O.E.D.); 4. 1. 19

CHRISTENDOM, christian name. A favourite expression with Nashe (cf. McKerrow, iii. 161. 12 'the right christendome of it is Cerdicke sands'). O.E.D. overlooks this meaning; 1. 1. 174

CITE, witness. A legal term = lit. to call witnesses; 1. 3. 207

CLEW, ball of thread or yarn; 1. 3. 179

CLOSE-STOOL, commode, 'a chamber utensil enclosed in a stool or box' (O.E.D.); 5. 2. 17

COARSELY, meanly, slightingly; 3. 5. 56

COIL, 'keep a coil' = make a fuss; 2. 1. 27

COMFORTABLE, lending moral or spiritual support; 1. 1. 77

COMMONER, prostitute; 5. 3. 193

COMPANION, fellow (in a contemptuous sense); 5. 3. 249

COMPANY, i.e. companion; 4. 3. 31

COMPOSITION, (i) product, combination; 1. 1. 203; (ii) bargain; 4. 3. 17

COMPT, reckoning; 5. 3. 57

CON THANKS, offer thanks, acknowledge gratitude; 4. 3. 149

CONDITION, nature, way of going on; 4. 3. 169, 253

CONGEE WITH, take leave of (cf. Fr. 'congé'); 4. 3. 85

CONVOY, means of transport, conveyance; 4. 3. 87; 4. 4. 10

CORAGIO!, courage!; 2. 5. 94

CORANTO, a lively dance (v. *Sh. Eng.* ii. 448–49); 2. 3. 46

COUNT OF, reckon with, attend to; 4. 3. 226

COX MY PASSION! A variant of 'Cock's passion' (cf. *Shrew,* 4. 1. 108), which is a corruption of 'God's passion'; 5. 2. 40–1

COZEN, cheat; 4. 2. 76; 4. 4. 23

CREATION, 'the investing with a title, dignity or function' (O.E.D.); 2. 3. 172

CREDIBLE, trustworthy; 1. 2. 4

CURIOUS, fastidious, difficult to please, minutely accurate; 1. 2. 20

CURIOUSLY, carefully, with cunning art; 4. 3. 32

CURTAL, a horse with its tail cut short—here used as a name; 2. 3. 62

CURTSY, bow, salute (not as now confined to the feminine bow); 3. 5. 90; 5. 3. 322

CURVET. Term of the manège = 'a leap of a horse in which the forelegs are raised together and equally advanced, and the hind-legs raised with a spring before the fore-legs reach the ground' (O.E.D.); 2. 3. 286

CUSTOMER, common woman, prostitute (cf. *Oth.* 4. 1. 123); 5. 3. 285

DEAR, severe, dire; 4. 5. 10

DEBILE, weak, 2. 3. 37

DEBOSHED, old form of 'debauched'; 2. 3. 141; 5. 3. 205

DEFAULT, 'in the d.' = at a need; 2. 3. 233

DELIVERANCE, manner of speech, speech; 2. 1. 82; 2. 5. 4

DERIVE, (i) inherit (cf. *well-derived*); 1. 1. 45; (ii) bring down upon (cf. *Hen. VIII*, 2. 4. 32 'What friend of mine/That had to him derived your anger, did I/Continue in my liking?'); 5. 3. 263

DIAL. May mean (i) a watch, (ii) a pocket sun-dial, or (iii) a mariner's compass; the last seems intended here; 2. 5. 6

DIET, (i) regulate to a fixed programme; 4. 3. 28; (ii) pay off after a day's work; 5. 3. 220

DIGEST, assimilate, amalgamate (cf. *Lear*, 1. 1. 130 'With my two daughters' dowers digest this third'); 5. 3. 74

DILATED, extended (an affected expression); 2. 1. 57

DILEMMAS. Meaning doubtful = either 'alternative courses of action' or 'difficulties to be faced'; 3. 6. 72

DISCIPLE, vb. teach, train; 1. 2. 28

DISSOLVE, discharge (cf. *M.W.W.* 5. 5. 215); 1. 2. 66

DISTANCE. A term of fencing = the interval to be kept between the combatants (cf. *R. & J.* 2. 4. 22; *M.W.W.* 2. 1. 201; and *L. Comp.* 151 'With safest distance I mine honour shielded'); 5. 3. 211

DISTEMPERED, inclement (of the weather); 1. 3. 148

DISTRACTED, torn asunder, divided; 5. 3. 35

DOCTRINE, science, knowledge; 1. 3. 238

DOLE, 'a portion sparingly doled out' (O.E.D.); 2. 3. 172

DONE, (a) lost, ruined (cf. *Ham.* 3. 2. 172; *V.A.* 197), (b) accomplished; 4. 2. 65

DOWER, one who gives a dowry to the bride (O.E.D. does not record this meaning); 4. 4. 19

DRUM, i.e. drummer; 5. 3. 252

DRUM (John or Tom). 'Tom Drum's entertainment' = a rough reception. There are many references to it in Eliz. literature; probably all go back to some anecdote now lost; 3. 6. 35; 5. 3. 320

EAR, plough; 1. 3. 43

EMBOSS, 'to drive a hunted animal to extremity' (O.E.D.); 3. 6. 95

EMBOWEL, i.e. disembowel; 1. 3. 238

EMPIRIC, quack; 2. 1. 122

ENGROSS, buy up wholesale, monopolise; 3. 2. 64

ENJOINED, 'enjoined penitents' = persons upon whom penance has been imposed by their spiritual director (cf. O.E.D. 'enjoin' 2); 3. 5. 92

ENSCONCE, lit. 'shelter within or behind a fortification (O.E.D.); 2. 3. 4.

ENTER (v. *well-entered*); 2. 1. 6

ENTERTAIN, engage, take into one's service; 4. 3. 87

ENTERTAINMENT, service; 3. 6. 11–12; 4. 1. 15

ESTEEM, sb. (a) value of a property, (b) reputation of a man; 5. 3. 1

EVEN, vb., adj., adv. The word is a commercial one and refers to the balancing of accounts (v. O.E.D. 'even' vb. 10); thus (i) 'to even' = to accomplish; 1. 3. 4; (ii) 'to make even' = to accomplish or carry out; 2. 1. 191 (v. note); and (iii) 'even truth' = completed or full truth; 5. 3. 324

EXAMINE, test, question closely; 3. 5. 62

EXCEPTION, disapproval (cf. mod. Eng. 'take exception'); 1. 2. 40

EXORCIST. Strictly speaking one who expels spirits, but commonly used at this period as synonymous with 'conjurer' = one who conjures or summons spirits; 5. 3. 303

EXPEDIENT, expeditious, swiftly performed; 2. 3. 182

FACINOROUS, infamous, abominably wicked; 2. 3. 32

FACT, crime; 3. 7. 47

FALL, decline, decadence; 2. 1. 13

FANCY, lit. fantasy, and so—a lover's fantasy, amorous inclination, love (in not a very serious sense); 5. 3. 213, 214

FATED, fateful, controlling the destinies of men; 1. 1. 216

FAVOUR, good looks, face, feature; 1. 1. 85, 98; 5. 3. 49

FEE-SIMPLE, an estate belonging to the owner and his heirs for ever; 4. 3. 274

FIGURE, astrological term = 'a scheme or table showing the disposition of the heavens at a given time' (O.E.D. 'figure' 14); 3. 1. 12

FILE, (i) roll, list; 3. 3. 9; (ii) file for letters; 4. 3. 201; (iii) rank, line of soldiers; 4. 3. 266

FIND, i.e. find out, unmask; 2. 3. 210; 2. 4. 32; 5. 2. 43

FINE, adj. subtle; 5. 3. 267

FINE, sb. end; 4. 4. 35; 5. 3. 214

FISNAMY (or 'fisnomy') = old form of 'physiognomy', face (v. note); 4. 5. 39

FISTULA, 'a long sinuous pipe-like ulcer with a narrow orifice' (O.E.D.); 1. 1. 35

FIT, to supply (e.g. with goods); 2. 1. 90

FLESH, to sate, gratify (lust); 4. 3. 15

FOLLOW, attend upon, wait on; 2. 1. 99

FOR, concerning; 2. 1. 45

FORE-PAST, already passed, previous (cf. Raleigh, *Discov. Guiana*, 21 'neither could any of the forepassed vndertakers...discouer the country'); 5. 3. 121

FORSAKE, (i) decline, refuse; 2. 3. 59; (ii) abandon, desert; 4. 2. 39

FRANK, (i) liberal, generous; 1. 2. 20; (ii) free; 2. 3. 58

FRENCH CROWN, (*a*) the coin paid to the 'taffeta punk', (*b*) the 'French disease' or syphilis; 2. 2. 21

FRIENDS, relations; 1. 3. 192

FURNISH TO, equip for; 2. 3. 294

FURNITURE, trappings; 2. 3. 62

GALEN, or Claudius Galenus (A.D. 131–? 200), the celebrated Greek physician, whose voluminous medical writings when translated into Latin in the 6th and 7th cents. acquired an authority which remained paramount in Europe for more than a thousand years. It was however challenged by Paracelsus (q.v.) in the 16th cent. and controversy followed which for a time split the medical profession into two schools, the Galenists and the Paracelsians; 2. 3. 12

GAMESTER, 'a lewd person, whether male or female' (O.E.D., cf. *Troil.* 4. 5. 63 'daughters of the game'); 5. 3. 187

GENERALLY, i.e. completely (cf. *Shrew*, 1. 2. 270 'generally beholding' = entirely beholden); 1. 1. 8

GO TO THE WORLD, get married (O.E.D. 'world' sb. 4c quotes from Calvin's *Sermons*, Eng. trans. 1579, 'This man is of the worlde, that is to say, he is married: This man is of the Churche, that is to say, Spirituall'): 1. 3. 18

GO UNDER, i.e. go under the name of, appear to be; 3. 5. 20

GOSSIP, vb. to be gossip or sponsor to, to give a name to (a 'gossip' = lit. god-kin, i.e. godfather or godmother); 1. 1. 175

GROAT, a coin equal to four pence; 2. 2. 20

GROSS, obvious, palpable; 1. 3. 169

GROSSLY, obviously; 1. 3. 175

HAND (in any), in any case (cf. *Shrew*, 1. 2. 144 'at any hand'; *L.L.L.* 4. 3. 215 'of all hands'); 3. 6. 38–9

HAWKING, keen as a hawk's; 1. 1. 96

HEEL (on the), at the end; 1. 2. 57

HELP (sb. & vb.), cure (freq. in Shakespeare); 1. 3. 235–6; 2. 1. 124, 189, 190; 2. 3. 18

HEN, a chicken-hearted person; 2. 3. 217

HERALDRY, rank, precedence; 2. 3. 267

HERB OF GRACE, or herb-grace, the old name for rue ('supposed to have arisen like the synonym, Herb of repentance, out of the formal coincidence of the name Rue with rue = repentance' O.E.D.); 4. 5. 16

HILDING, good-for-nothing (lit. a vicious horse); 3. 6. 3

HOLD, i.e. uphold (v. note 1. 1. 9); 1. 1. 9, 79; 2. 3. 231; 3. 2. 89

HOLDING, consistency, coherence (cf. 1 *Hen. IV*, 1, 2, 34 'Thou sayest well, and it holds well too'); 4. 2. 27

HOME, adv. (i) completely, effectively; 5. 3. 4; (ii) back again to its right place; 5. 3. 222

HONESTY, chastity; *passim*

HOODMAN, the blind-man in 'hoodman-blind' or blind-man's-buff; 4. 3. 116

HOST, vb. lodge, put up; 3. 5. 92

IDLE, foolish, cracked, delirious; 2. 5. 51; 3. 7. 26

IMAGE, representative; 2. 1. 198

IMPORTANT, urgent, importunate, not to be withstood (cf. *Err.* 5. 1. 138; *Ado*, 2. 1. 63); 3. 7. 21

IMPORTING, important; 5. 3. 136

IMPOSITION, a task laid upon one; 4. 4. 29

INCLINING, partiality, favouritism; 3. 6. 35–6

INDUCEMENT, instigation, influence; 3. 2. 87

INGENEROUS, dastardly; 5. 2. 23

INHIBITED, forbidden; 1. 1. 146–7

INN, vb. gather in grain, harvest; 1. 3. 44

INNOCENT, imbecile; 4. 3. 184

INSTANCE, evidence; 4. 1. 40

INTEEMABLE, incapable of being emptied, inexhaustible; 1. 3. 199

INTER'GATORY. A legal expression = 'a question formally put, or drawn up in writing to be put, to an accused person or witness' (O.E.D.); 4. 3. 180

JADE, a sorry nag; 2. 3. 288; 'jades' tricks' = mischievous tricks; 4. 5. 60

JOWL, vb. to dash or knock (two heads) together; 1. 3. 53

JUSTIFY, make good, confirm, prove; 4. 3. 52

KICKY-WICKY, 'a jocular or ludicrous term for a wife' (O.E.D., which suggests that it may be a humorous formation after the pattern of 'kicksy-winsey' = whim or erratic fancy); 2. 3. 284

KIND (in their), in their own way; 1. 3. 176

KNOWINGLY, i.e. with knowledge to justify one's opinion; 1. 3. 247

LASE, fall, ruin; 2. 3. 166

LATTICE (window of), 'a window of lattice-work (usually painted red), or a pattern on the shutter or wall imitating this, formerly a common mark of an ale-house or inn' (O.E.D.); 2. 3. 217

LAY, exorcise or calm (a disturbed spirit); 4. 3. 18

LEAGUER, camp; 3. 6. 24

LEAVE OFF, give up as incurable (cf. O.E.D. 'leave' 14c (*b*)); 1. 3. 238

LEVEL, aim, the act of taking aim, the mark at which the weapon is aimed; 2. 1. 156

LIME, to catch with bird-lime (a glutinous substance smeared upon twigs to take small birds); 3. 5. 23

LING (old), salted ling (O.E.D. quotes a cookery book of 1747, 'old ling, which is the best sort of salt fish'), commonly eaten in Lent; 3. 2. 13, 14

LINSEY-WOOLSEY, lit. coarse material, part wool part flax. Hence —neither one thing nor another, a medley, nonsense; 4. 1. 11

LIST, lit. border, edge, strip. Hence—limit, boundary; 2. 1. 52

LIVELIHOOD, animation. The word is found once elsewhere in Sh. (i.e. *V.A.* 26); 1. 1. 52

'LONGING, belonging; 4. 2. 42

LOSE, orig. meaning = to ruin. Hence—to ruin in estimation (cf. O.E.D. 'lose' 2b); 5. 2. 44

LOUSY, contemptible, of no importance (cf. fig. use of 'scurvy' and 2 *Hen. VI*, 4. 1. 50 (F) 'Obscure and lousy swain'); 4. 3. 191

LOVE-LINE, love-letter; 2. 1. 78

LUSTICK, an exclamation inviting joviality, well known in 17th c., quibbling on 'lusty'; 2. 3. 44

MADE, i.e. a made man (cf. *Oth.* 1. 2. 51 'he's made for ever'); 4. 3. 17

MAGNANIMOUS, very valiant; 3. 6. 63

MEASURE, dance; 2. 1. 56

MEDICINE, (i) a physician; 2. 1. 72, (ii) alchemical drugs, the elixir of life or philosopher's stone (cf. licence of 1456, quoted *Sh. Eng.* i. 465 'In former times wise and famous philosophers in their writings and books have left on record and taught under figures and coverings that from wine, precious stones, oils, vegetables, animals, metals, and minerals can be made many glorious and notable medicines, and chiefly that most precious medicine which some philosophers have called the mother and Empress of medicines, others the priceless glory, others the quintessence, others the Philosopher's Stone and Elixir of Life'); 5. 3. 102

MELL, vb. to have sexual intercourse; 4. 3. 225

MERE, absolute, plain; 3. 5. 54

MERELY, absolutely, altogether; 4. 3. 20

METTLE, the stuff of life, the substance out of which man is made (cf. *Macb.* 1. 7. 73–4 'thy undaunted mettle should compose nothing but males,' and *Meas.* G.); 1. 1. 131

MISPRISE, despise, depreciate; 3. 2. 30

MISPRISION, (a) contempt—cf. *misprise*, (b) i.e. mis-prison, false imprisonment (cf. 'shackle up'); 2. 3. 155

MODERN, commonplace; 2. 3. 2; 5. 3. 215

MODULE, pattern (lit. architect's plan). The word is of different origin from 'model' but the two forms are used indiscriminately in Sh.; 4. 3. 97

MOIETY, share; 3. 2. 65

MONUMENTAL, (a) memorial—cf. 3. 7. 22–5, (b) serving to identify ('monument' = sign, token, cf. *Shrew*, 3. 2. 93); 4. 3. 16

MOOD, anger (cf. *Two Gent.* 4. 1. 51 'Whom in my mood, I stabbed unto the heart'); 5. 2. 4

MOTION, (i) speed; 2. 3. 238; (ii) action; 3. 1. 13; (iii) suggestion, proposal; 5. 3. 262

MOTIVE, something or somebody that causes another thing or person to move; 4. 4. 20; 5. 3. 214

MUSE, wonder; 2. 5. 67

MUSK-CAT, or musk-deer, the animal from which musk is procured; 5. 2. 20

MUSTER-FILE, muster-roll; 4. 3. 163

MYSTERY, skill, art; 3. 6. 61

NATURALIZE, familiarise; 1. 1. 208

NATURE, character, disposition, (here perhaps) rank (cf. Jonson, *E. Man in H.* 5. 3. 138, Herford & Simpson, *Works*, iii. 279 'vncase & appeare in mine owne proper nature, seruant to this gentleman'); 3. 1. 17

NAUGHTY, worthless; 5. 3. 252

NE = and not (an archaic form not found elsewhere in Sh. except *Per.* 2. prol. 36); 2. 1. 173

NESSUS, the Centaur who ravished Deianira, bride of Hercules; 4. 3. 247

NEXT, nearest; 1. 3. 58

NOTE, distinction; 1. 3. 154

OFFICE (rb.), act as a servant, 'run' a house (cf. *Wint.* 1. 2. 172); 3. 2. 125

OR, before (cf. *Ham.* 5. 2. 30 (Q2) 'Or I could make a prologue'); 1. 3. 85

ORDINARY, 'a public meal regularly provided at a fixed price in an eating-house or tavern' (O.E.D.); 2. 3. 205

OUTWARD, without inside knowledge; 3. 1. 11

OWE, own; 2. 1. 9; 2. 5. 81; 3. 2. 118

PACE, the short walking steps of a horse when trained (N.B. the contrast with '*runs* where he will'); 4. 5. 66

PALMER, pilgrim. The 'palmer' was strictly speaking a special kind of pilgrim, but no special significance seems intended here; 3. 5. 34

PARACELSUS (c. 1493–1541), the famous Swiss alchemist and physician, who applied his chemical knowledge to the traditional pharmacy and therapeutics, and attacked orthodox medical opinion which derived from Galen (q.v.); 2. 3. 12

PARCEL, small party (cf. *M.V.* 1. 2. 103); 2. 3. 55

PASS, reputation; 2. 5. 55

PASSAGE, (*a*) phrase, expression, (*b*) passing-away; 1. 1. 19

PASSPORT, an official document issued by town corporations or J.P.s giving beggars permission to ask alms and specifying the route they were allowed to take from one town to another; 3. 2. 55

PERSPECTIVE, lit. any kind of optical instrument for viewing objects, but 'in early use applied to various optical devices, as arrangements of mirrors etc. for producing some special or fantastic effect, e.g. by distortion of images' (O.E.D.). Cf. *Sh. Eng.* ii. 10 for the portrait of Edward VI painted in perspective; 5. 3. 48

PHŒNIX, paragon, unique person; 1. 1. 168

PILE, (*a*) the downy nap on velvet or other fabrics. Velvets were cut in three heights; 'two pile and a half' therefore = something a little less than the best velvet; (*b*) ? quibble upon 'piled' = pilled or peeled, i.e. hairless as a result of the 'French disease' (cf. *Meas.* G.); 4. 5. 96

PILOT'S GLASS. Some have supposed that Shakespeare erred in making the nautical glass an hour and not a half-hour glass; but v. *Sh. Eng.* i. 164, and cf. *Temp.* G.; 2. 1. 165

PIN-BUTTOCK, narrow or pointed buttock; 2. 2. 17

PLACE (take), take effect, succeed, find acceptance; 1. 1. 105

PLAUSIVE, plausible; 4. 1. 26

PLUCK, draw (in cards). Cf. Fletcher, *Custom of the Country*, 1. 1. 'Would any man stand plucking for the ace of hearts, with one pack, of cards, all days on's life?' (v. O.E.D. 'pluck' vb. 2 d); 1. 3. 87

PLUTUS, the god of gold, and therefore the god of alchemists (v. note); 5. 3. 101

POLL, the number of soldiers in the muster (cf. *Cor.* 3. 1. 134); 4. 3. 164

PORT, gate; 3. 5. 35

PREDOMINANT. A predominant star was one in the ascendant, i.e. in that degree of the Zodiac which at any given moment (esp. at child-birth) is just rising above the horizon (v. O.E.D. 'ascendant' B. i. 1); 1. 1. 197

PRETENCE, design, intention; 4. 3. 36

PRIME, youth; 2. 1. 182

PROFESSION, i.e. what one professes; 2. 1. 83

PROPER, own; 4. 2. 49

PROPERTY, particular quality; 2. 1. 187

PUDDING, sausage; 2. 2. 26

PUNK, harlot; 2. 2. 21

PUR, the name of the knave in the card-game 'post and pair'; 5. 2. 19

PUT OFF, (*a*) brush aside, (*b*) palm off (lit. 'dispose of fraudulently,' v. O.E.D. 'put' 45 k); 2. 2. 6, 9

QUALITY, rank, social position; 1. 3. 111

QUATCH-BUTTOCK. The only recorded instance of 'quatch': probably = quat, i.e. fat; 2. 2. 17

QUESTANT. A Shakespearian coinage from 'quest' = (of hunting dogs) 'to search for game' O.E.D. Cf. *Meas.* 4. 1. 61 'Run with these false and most contrarious quests,' where 'quests' = the cry of hounds upon the trail; 2. 1. 16

QUIRKS, ups and downs. The orig. meaning of 'quirk' seems to have been 'a flourish or sudden twist or turn in writing or drawing' (v. O.E.D.); 3. 2. 48

QUIT, (*a*) absolve, acquit, cf. *Hen. V*, 2. 2. 166 'God quit you in his mercy,' (*b*) pay him back; 5. 3. 298

QUOTED, well-known, notorious; 5. 3. 204

REAVE, rob by force; 5. 3. 86

REBELLION, irresistible desire, outbreak of lust. This meaning, not recorded in O.E.D., is common in Shakespeare (cf. *Meas.* 3. 2. 112; 2 *Hen. IV*, 2. 4. 380; *M.V.* 3. 1. 33 'Out upon it, old carrion, rebels it at these years?'); 4. 3. 18; 5. 3. 6

RECTOR, ruler, governor (cf. *Cor.* 2. 3. 213); 4. 3. 56

RELICS, mementoes, souvenirs (cf. *Jul. Caes.* 2. 2. 89 'Great men shall press for tinctures, stains, relics and cognizance'); 1. 1. 100; 5. 3. 25

REMAINDER, interest in an estate coming into effect upon the death of a legatee; 4. 3. 276

REMOVE, departure from one place to another; 5. 3. 131

RENDER, represent, describe, report (cf. *A.Y.L.* 4. 3. 122); 1. 3. 227

REPEAL, recall from exile (cf. *R. II*, 2. 2. 49 'The banished Bolingbroke repeals himself'); 2. 3. 52

RESIDENCE, continuance in a course of action (v. O.E.D. 'residence' 3); 2. 5. 41

RESOLVEDLY, i.e. until everything is explained; 5. 3. 330

RESPECTS, reasons; 2. 5. 68

REST, 'set up one's rest,' i.e. to be determined, resolved. The expression, derived from the card-game primero, in which the 'rest' was the name for the reserved stakes, originally meant 'to hazard one's all'; 2. 1. 135

RETROGRADE. 'A retrograde star was one apparently moving in a direction contrary to the order of the signs of the Zodiac, or from east to west' O.E.D., quoting Culpepper 'If a planet retrograde...he denotes much discord and contradiction in the business'; 1. 1. 198

RIDDLE-LIKE, mysteriously; 1. 3. 214

RING-CARRIER, go-between; 3. 5. 90

RUFF, or ruffle, 'the loose turned-over portion or flap of a top-boot' (O.E.D. 'ruffle'). It is possible that 'ruff' is a misp. for 'ruffle', but it is also possible that 'ruff' and 'ruffle' were used interchangeably; 3. 2. 7

RUTTISH, lecherous; 4. 3. 212

SADNESS, seriousness; 4. 3. 200

SAUCY, (i) insolent, impertinent; 2. 3. 265; (ii) wanton, lascivious; 4. 4. 23

SCIENCE, profound knowledge; 5. 3. 103

SCORE, to obtain drink, goods, etc. on credit (O.E.D. 'score' 11, quoting Heywood, *Fair Maid of West*, 1. 12 'It is the commonest thing that can bee for these Captaines to score and to score, but when the scores are to be paid, Non est inventus'); 4. 3. 221

SEASON, 'to preserve by salting' (Malone); 1. 1. 49

SENSE, (i) perception, apprehension; 1. 3. 169; (ii) reason; 2. 1. 124

SET DOWN, lay siege (cf. *Cor.* 4. 7. 28 'All places yield to him ere he sets down'); 1. 1. 120

SHREWD, (i) 'a shrewd turn' = a nasty trick; 3. 5. 67, (ii) keen-witted (cf. *Troil.* 1. 2. 206); 4. 5. 62

SHREWDLY, grievously; 3. 5. 87

SHRIEVE, old form of 'sheriff'; 4. 3. 184

SMOKE, smell out, suspect; 3. 6. 98; 4. 1. 27

SNIPT-TAFFETA, slashed silk. Taffeta = thin silken stuff of lustrous appearance; masks and vizards were commonly made from it, which perhaps accounts for its frequent use in expressions denoting at once dressiness and lack of substance (cf. *L.L.L.* 5. 2. 406 'Taffeta phrases, silken terms precise'); 4. 5. 1–2

SNUFF, (a) a wick on the point of extinction; a feeble old man, (b) something offensive to the nose (cf. 'take it in snuff' = take offence, 1 *Hen. IV*, 1. 3. 41); 1. 2. 59

SOLEMN, ceremonial; 2. 3. 273

SQUARE, to frame or adjust something according to some standard or principle. A metaphor from stone- or wood-work; 2. 1. 150

STAGGERS, giddiness, 2. 3. 166

STAIN, a dash or touch; 1. 1. 113

STALL, keep. A metaphor from the stable not found elsewhere in Shakespeare; 1. 3. 123

STAND FOR, stand up for, fight for; 1. 1. 135

START, alarm, startle; 5. 3. 231

STICK, fix, pin (like an ornament); 5. 3. 45

SUBSCRIBE FOR, undertake on behalf of; 4. 5. 31

SUCCEEDING, i.e. consequences; 2. 3. 194

SUGGEST, tempt (as often in Shakespeare); 4. 5. 44

SUGGESTION, temptation; 3. 5. 17

SUITED, clothed, apparelled; 1. 1. 158

TABLE, lit. 'a board or flat surface on which a picture was painted; hence, the picture itself' (O.E.D.); 1. 1. 97

TAFFETY, i.e. dressed in silk or taffeta (v. *snipt-taffeta*); 2. 2. 21

TAKE OFF, relieve one of; 2. 1. 89

TAKE PLACE (v. *place*); 1. 1. 105

TAKE UP, (a) pick up, (b) enlist; v. note; 2. 3. 211

TAX, blame, reprove; 1. 1. 69; 2. 1. 170; 5. 3. 122, 205

THICK!, i.e. quick!; 2. 2. 43

TIME (in happy), i.e. Fortune favours us!; 5. 1. 6

TITLE, i.e. what one is worth, lit. that to which one has a title; 2. 4. 26

TOLL, to get rid of, lit. to enter for sale on the toll-book of a market (cf. Bacon, *Use Com. Law*, 'If hee bee a horse hee must be ridden two houres in the market or faire…and tolled for in the toll-book'); 5. 3. 147

TOOTH, appetite; 2. 3. 45

TOP (forward), forelock. The orig. meaning of 'top' (v. O.E.D.). 'To take by the top' = to seize

by the hair, lay hold of by main force; 5. 3. 39

TOUCH, feeling, emotion of a subtle kind (cf. *Temp.* 5. 1. 21; *Two Gent.* 2. 7. 18); 1. 3. 115

TRICK, 'a characteristic expression (of the face or voice), a peculiar feature, a distinguishing trait' O.E.D. (cf. *John*, 1. 1. 85 'He hath a trick of Cœur-de-lion's face,' and *Lear*, 4. 6. 108 'The trick of that voice I do well remember'); 1. 1. 98

TRIPLE, one of three, third (cf. *A. & C.* 1. 1. 12 'The triple pillar of the world'); 2. 1. 108

TWIGS, covered with lime (q.v.) to catch birds; 3. 6. 101

VALIDITY, worth; 5. 3. 191

VENT, 'make vent of' = talk of (cf. *V. A.* 334 'Free vent of words love's fire doth assuage'); 2. 3. 206

WEAR, sb. fashion; 1. 1. 205

WEAR, vb. to be in the fashion; 1. 1. 159; 2. 1. 53

WEIGH, rate, estimate; 3. 4. 32

WELL-DERIVED, i.e. of a good stock (cf. *derive*); 3. 2. 86

WELL-ENTERED, thoroughly initiated, well trained (O.E.D. quotes Udall, 1548, 'Sounde meate for such as are wel entred'); 2. 1. 6

WELL-FOUND, 'of tried merit' (O.E.D.); 2. 1. 102

WILL, lust; 4. 3. 15

WIND (have i'th'), have scent of; 3. 6. 108

WOODCOCK, gull, dupe, fool (in allusion to the ease with which the woodcock could be snared); 4. 1. 90

WORLD (go to the), v. *Go to the world*; 1. 3. 18
WORTHY; merited; 4. 3. 7
WRACK, old form of 'wreck'; 3. 5. 22
WRITE, to attain to, (i) 'to write man' = to reach man's estate; 2. 3 201; (ii) 'writ as little beard' = attained to as little beard (in allusion to the stock phrase 'to write man'); 2. 3. 64

WORDSWORTH CLASSICS

General Editors: Marcus Clapham and Clive Reynard
Titles in this series

DISTRIBUTION

AUSTRALIA, BRUNEI
& MALAYSIA
Treasure Press
22 Salmon Street, Port Melbourne
Vic 3207, Australia
Tel: (03) 646 6716
Fax (03) 646 6925

DENMARK
BOG-FAN
St. Kongensgade 61A
1264 København K

BOGPA SIKA
Industrivej 1, 7120 Vejle Ø

FRANCE
Bookking International
16 Rue des Grands Augustins
75006 Paris

GERMANY, AUSTRIA
& SWITZERLAND
Swan Buch-Marketing GmbH
Goldscheuerstrabe 16
D-7640 Kehl Am Rhein, Germany

GREAT BRITAIN & IRELAND
Wordsworth Editions Ltd
Cumberland House, Crib Street,
Ware, Hertfordshire SG12 9ET

Selecta Books
The Selectabook
Distribution Centre
Folly Road, Roundway, Devizes
Wiltshire SN10 2HR

RUSSIA & CHINA
UPC Consulting
Wolffinite 36
65200 Vaasa
Finland

HOLLAND & BELGIUM
Uitgeverlj en Boekhandel
Van Gennep BV, Spuistraat 283
1012 VR Amsterdam, Holland

INDIA
OM Book Service
1690 First Floor
Nai Sarak, Delhi – 110006
Tel: 3279823-3265303 Fax: 3278091

ITALY
Magis Books
Piazza Della Vittoria I/C
42100 Reggio Emilia
Tel: 0522-452303 Fax: 0522-452845

NEW ZEALAND
Whitcoulls Limited
Private Bag 92098, Auckland

NORTH AMERICA
Universal Sales & Marketing
230 Fifth Avenue, Suite 1212
New York, New York 10001
Fax: 212-481-3534

NORWAY
Norsk Bokimport AS
Bertrand Narvesensvei 2
Postboks 6219, Etterstad, 0602 Oslo

SINGAPORE
Book Station
18 Leo Drive, Singapore
Tel: 4511998 Fax: 4529188

SOUTH AFRICA, ZIMBABWE
CENTRAL & E. AFRICA
Trade Winds Press (Pty) Ltd
P O Box 20194, Durban North 4016

SPAIN
Libreria Ribera
Dr. Areilza No.19, 48011 Bilbao
Tel: 441-87-87 Fax: 441-80-29

SWEDEN
Akademibokhandelsgruppen
Box 21002, 100 31 Stockholm

DIRECT MAIL
Jay Communications Ltd
Redvers House, 13 Fairmile,
Henley-on-Thames, Oxfordshire RG9 2JR
Tel: 0491 572656 Fax: 0491 573590